# CLASSIC MOMENTS
## OF
# ATHLETICS

*Classic Moments of*

# ATHLETICS

**MOORLAND PUBLISHING**  Moorland Publishing Co Ltd
P.O. Box 2
Ashbourne Derbyshire England
DE6 1DZ
Telephone 0335 44486

*With Compliments*

and Congratulations

*Charles Landon*

Title page: Alan Wells (G.B.) on the
starting blocks
Rear Cover: Steve Ovett

British Library Cataloguing in Publication Data

Landon, Charles
    Classic moments of athletics
    1. Athletics — History
    I. Title
    796.4        GV1060.5

    ISBN 0 86190 053 7

The author wishes to thank John Grainger who compiled
the index for this book.

ISBN 0 86190 053 7

Printed in the U.K. by
Butler and Tanner Ltd, Frome
for Moorland Publishing Company Ltd,
PO Box 2, 9-11 Station Street, Ashbourne,
Derbyshire, DE6 1DZ, England

# CONTENTS

# ILLUSTRATIONS

**Picture Sources.** Illustrations have been provided by: John Grainger Picture Agency: p 16, 19, 22, 23, 28, 30, 32, 33, 35, 36, 37, 45, 53, 74, 92, 93; Keystone Press Agency: p 17, 25, 39, 51, 55, 57, 61, 62, 63, 67, 70, 73, 76, 78, 80, 82, 84, 86, 96, 97, 101, 102, 104, 107, 110, 112, 118, 121, 126, 131; Provincial Sports Photography: p 90, 115, 117, 122, 125, 134, 136.

# INTRODUCTION

'Serious sport has nothing to do with fair play. It is bound up with hatred, jealousy, boastfulness, disregard of all rules and sadistic pleasure in witnessing violence. In other words, it is war minus the shooting.' So wrote George Orwell in 1950, and those who visit a soccer ground on any Saturday of the winter season would be hard put to disagree with that assessment. But athletics . . . well, that is something different is it not? The sight of clean-limbed young men and women running, jumping and throwing has always conjured up images of those Olympians of ancient times. Even those cynics who point out that, at international level at least, there is probably just as much 'gamesmanship' in athletics as in any other sport, would be hard pressed to argue that track and field athletics is not a family sport to be enjoyed by all.

It seems that athletics, in one form or another, has always been with us. In Ancient Greece, of course, there were the Olympic Games, revived in their modern form in 1896. In Britain, we learn that in the year 1365, Edward III banned 'weight putting' for fear that it might prevent archery practice. In Mrs Elizabeth Gaskell's *The Life of Charlotte Brontë*, published in 1857, we are told: 'Scarcely a wedding took place without the rough amusement of foot races where the half-naked runners were a scandal to decent strangers.' Indeed, it seems that men have run, jumped and thrown in competition against each other for thousands of years.

As far back as 1829BC — four and a half centuries before the Olympic Games are believed to have begun in Greece — the Tailteann Games in Ireland were taking place. After the Olympics died in AD393, the sport of athletics as we know it slid into a vague kind of competition until in the nineteenth century, athletics became popular and more organised. The Royal Military Academy at Sandhurst organised competitions before the first athletic club in the world — the Necton Guild of Norfolk, (no mention of it is made after 1826) — was formed in 1817.

Since then the sport has progressed apace. In 1839, a meeting was held in Toronto and it is believed this was the first such event on the North American continent. In 1862 the first amateur open meeting was held in England; and two years later the annual Oxford-Cambridge match was staged for the first time, the Exeter College (Oxford) Athletic Club having been in existence since 1850 and thus the oldest surviving club today. In 1866 the Amateur Athletic Club was formed 'to afford all classes of gentlemen amateurs the means of competing against one another without being compelled to mix with professional runners'. In 1876 the American Championships were held for the first time and that same year there was the first record of international competition when London Athletic Club (formed as Mincing Lane Athletic Club in 1863 and

renamed six years later) was responsible for an England team competing in Ireland. There followed all manner of milestones — the formation of the Amateur Athletic Association and its championships in 1880, the establishment of the International Amateur Athletic Federation in 1913, the Women's AAA in 1922, the Commonwealth Games (then also carrying the 'Empire' title) in 1930, the European Championships in 1934, and the World Cup Tournament in 1977. There are, too, the Asian Games (begun in New Delhi in 1951), and the African Games (started in the Congo in 1965).

With all these competitions have come innovations undreamed of by the athletes of other eras. There are the all-weather tracks, the improvements in sports equipment — glass fibre vaulting poles and aerodynamic javelins to name but two, photo-finish equipment and electronic timing devices; and there have been the technical improvements of people like the Americans Parry O'Brien (in the shot) and Dick Fosbury (in the high jump) which have opened up new heights — and distances — to athletes. That, of course, leads us to what makes athletics the great sport it is — the athletes themselves. The names ring down the years — George, Nurmi, Owens, Blankers-Koen, Zatopek, Kuts, Bannister, and the rest. They are what makes this sport so fascinating, exciting, at times wondrous.

In the past they perhaps viewed the sport differently from today when athletes train almost full-time. Joe Binks, the British mile record-holder of 1902, is reported to have trained for about half an hour each week; Douglas Lowe, who was twice the Olympic 800 metres champion in 1924 and 1928, reckoned that 'three times training a week at the most should suffice'; and even the legendary Sydney Wooderson, holder of the world mile record before World War II, said, 'I used to take a whole month off.' But they were all dedicated, however light their training schedules seem to us today. One thing is certain: men and women will continue to strive for faster times, greater heights and distances; they will carry on looking for new peaks to conquer. The limit of human endurance has not been reached yet. As they do so they will continue to produce classic moments of athletics.

The object of this book is to record some of those moments. Even as it is being produced, athletes will be breaking some of the records mentioned, endeavouring to perform their own classic performances. In a relatively short time, new chapters will have to be added. But the deeds already done will have lost none of their appeal for all that. Many runners now take less than four minutes to run a mile — but Bannister's run at Iffley Road in May 1954 was, is, and always will be a classic. So will they all.

# EARLY HEROES OF TRACK AND FIELD

On a rainy Saturday afternoon in the summer of 1880, a tall, lean, haggard man in a long black running costume stood at the starting line of the running track at the Lillie Bridge Athletic Ground in West London. Rain hammered against his face, streamed down his neck, and dripped from his drooping moustache. The man jogged up and down on the line, made a vain attempt to blow the rain from his mouth, and then surveyed his chest and legs encased in the running costume which clung heavily to his skin. Huddled under the covered grandstand some 1,200 people watched as the starter, dressed in a frock-coat and a silk hat, lowered his umbrella and fired a starting pistol. Walter

Walter George of Moseley Harriers who became the first AAA Champion when he won the mile, unopposed in 1880. George was Britain's first great amateur runner in distances of a mile and over, though despite breaking a dozen world records as an amateur, it was a professional mile race against the Scotsman, William Cummings, in 1886 which ensured his legendary status. George won in 4min 12.8sec – and not until 1915 did any athlete, amateur or professional, do better.

Goodall George, a 21-year-old son of Wiltshire, began his lonely run around the track. For one mile George splashed alone until he passed the tape four minutes and twenty-eight and six-tenths of a second later. Walter George, the man who no one would race against that day — 3 July 1880 — thus became the first Amateur Athletic Association champion.

George's prowess as a runner, particularly as a miler, is recorded later in this book, in a chapter devoted to the eventual running of the first sub-four minute mile by Roger Bannister in 1954. But he has to be mentioned here, also, as one of the great heroes of the nineteenth-century athletics arena, and particularly since he was the first man to win an AAA Championship. There was no ceremony to herald the start of what was to become over a century of such events. Indeed, it was only the luck of the draw that decreed Walter George should be remembered thus. The lack of any opposition was due to the fact that it had been rumoured that George had run 4min 20sec in training — and at a time when the amateur record stood at 4min 24.5sec, none of the other contenders of the time were keen to risk being so severely outdone. George went on to many great feats including in both 1882 and 1884, winning four AAA Championships — the 880 yards, 1 mile, 4 miles and 10 miles. He was one of the first of many classic athletes to have tasted their first successes at the AAAs.

The history of the Amateur Athletic Association and its Championships has already been well documented in great detail. Throughout those records there are the great athletes and their epic feats, for if rain ruined the first competition in 1880, a competition which was largely unmemorable apart from the historical significance of the event, then it was not a harbinger of what was to follow. The following year, the sun shone brilliantly, the crowd now numbered over 12,000, and the second AAA Championships became a legend in Victorian sport. This time the Championships were held at Birmingham's Aston Lower Grounds — one of the prime factors in the AAA's foundation was that the Championships should rotate from the South to the Midlands and the North — and the crowds had flocked to see two Americans, Lawrence Myers and E.E. Merrill, whose feats on their tour of England had already caught the imagination of the Victorians.

A riot in Merrill's previous race — a one mile walk — had ensued after the local favourite had been disqualified on this very track. Now there was a strong police presence as Myers and Merrill prepared for the afternoon's events. Myers was the first into action, in the first heat of the opening event, the 100 yards. A sickly-looking 23-year-old whose mother had died of tuberculosis, Myers was nevertheless the champion of the United States at every distance from 100 yards to 880 yards — and also held the Canadian titles the same year — as well as breaking every American record from 100 yards to one mile. A bad start cost Myers the

*Walter Snook, the Moseley Harrier who won eight AAA titles as well as the national cross-country championship. In 1886, Snook received his second suspension, this time permanently, for alleged infringements of the rules governing professionalism and betting.*

race and when he was eliminated in the very first heat, finishing fourth, there were knowing glances from the British. The Australian, Bernhard Wise, in his last appearance for Oxford University, won the mile from George, with the favourite, William Snook, dropping out to save himself for the four miles. There followed the seven-miles walk, but again there was disaster for the Americans. Liverpool wheelwright, Harry Webster, was disqualified after three miles. Henry Whyatt, the local man whose disqualification had caused a near-riot here the week before dropped out, and the field was left to Merrill and a lad from Elland, Yorkshire. Then Merrill fainted and the novice Yorkshireman, James Raby, finished the second half of the race alone.

But America's day was to come on this astonishing day. At the start of the 440 yards, Lawrence Myers, in his knee-length running costume and headscarf knotted at the neck, limbered up alongside big William Phillips, the 100 yards champion of that year and of the inaugural championships. Phillips went straight into the lead and gained a three-yard advantage over the American. But Myers was not to be outdone. He had a bizarre style, running with arms dangling loosely at his side, letting his long stride do all the work. It looked so comical to the British who had seen nothing like it. Then, into the back straight, Myers suddenly swept into the lead. He surged past Phillips to win in 48.6 seconds. It was a shattering blow to the British hopes and one of the most sensational performances ever seen on a British track. The best quarter-miler that England could produce had to suffer the ignominy of having the American turn and beckon him on as if to say, 'Come on, let's make a real race of it!' The British record of 50.4 seconds remained, so far as the sole arbiters, the press, were concerned, due to the uneveness of the awkward Aston track — a lap was 501 yards (458.4 metres) — but nothing can detract from Myers's amazing run.

There were more sensations to come. In the pole vault — or 'pole jump' as it was then known, Tom Ray, a nineteen-year-old from the Lake District, set a new world record of 3.43 metres (11ft 3in). He might have gone higher, but for the fact that the posts ended there! Back on the track there were still more great performances. In the four miles, eighteen-year-old George Nehan led three world record holders. Walter George (mile record-holder) and William Snook (two miles) failed to finish in the face of the blistering pace; and George Dunning (fifteen-miles record-holder) was over fifty yards behind at the post. Nehan's time of 20min 26.2sec was a Championship record. Only cramp robbed him of further glory in the ten miles on the following Monday when he dropped out after two miles.

In 1885, William Snook emulated the feat performed twice by Walter George and took four titles at the AAA Championships — mile, 4 miles, 10 miles and 2 mile steeplechase — and from then until the outbreak of World War I there were many great names who contributed their own classic performances to these early days of athletics. In 1886 Arthur Wharton, the first West Indian-born athlete to win an AAA title, took the 100 yards in evens — his ten-second sprint setting a new British record. Curiously, Wharton was a professional goalkeeper with Preston North End, though the AAA had ruled in 1883 that professional cricketers could not enter amateur athletics events. Professional soccer was not added to the blacklist until 1899. So Wharton ran in his own right, though Snook, eventually winner of eight AAA titles, had already been suspended. The world record-holder for two miles had been banned until the end of 1882 for being involved in the entry of a professional runner in an amateur race in Lancashire. In 1886, Snook was suspended again, this time permanently, for allegedly allowing J.E. Hickman of Godiva Harriers to win the national cross country championship. The bookmakers had made Snook the hot favourite and the implications were obvious. Snook appealed several times but failed to be reinstated. It was one of the sensations of Victorian athletics. The cir-

cumstantial evidence pointed to the fact that Snook was not trying. At twenty-five years of age he was finished as an amateur athlete — and at the time he was the greatest English distance runner.

Sadly, several of the best athletes around the end of the nineteenth century were involved in incidents which took the limelight away from their own achievements. Betting was one 'evil', the payment of money to amateurs to induce them to appear in certain meetings was another. In the wake of Snook, George — who had turned professional quite legitimately — and the others, it took some years for English distance running to recover. When it did, it was a man called Alfred Shrubb who set the sport alight once more with several stunning runs. Shrubb's record was quite phenomenal and contained several classic performances. Yet he, too, was to fall foul of the authorities over payment of expenses.

Shrubb was a brilliant runner — AAA 1 mile champion 1903-4, 4 miles 1901-4, and 10 miles 1901-4, as well as national cross-country champion 1901-4, and international champion 1903-4. Shrubb's talent was such that he held almost every British record from one and a half miles to one hour. Many of his records lasted for thirty years and one for as long as forty-nine years. His world records, too, enjoyed great longevity. His ten-miles record of 50min 40.6sec was not bettered for twenty-four years, his two-miles record of 9min 9.6sec for twenty-two years, three-miles (14min 17.2sec) for eighteen years, one-hour record of 18,742 metres for nine years, six miles (29min 59.4sec) and 10,000 metres (31min 2.4sec) for seven years. Consider also that all these records were set in one year — 1904 — though Shrubb was denied certain Olympic gold medals because Britain did not send a team to St Louis. Early in 1905, Shrubb toured New Zealand and Australia at the expense of the New Zealand AAA and set a number of national records. Shrubb was prevented by the AAA from accepting invitations to Canada and South Africa the same year — the invitations had arrived at the AAA offices where it was decided to refuse them on the runner's behalf — and Shrubb, angry at what he felt was arrogant treatment, went to Canada anyway. In September 1905, Shrubb was suspended over allegations concerning travel expenses. In November, a newspaper article made further allegations over his expenses and after two special meetings he was permanently suspended. Like most of the others who had experienced this fate he became a professional, one of his most bizarre contests after that being a series of ten-mile races against a horse. In the 1920s this great distance runner, probably the greatest of his era, became Oxford University's first professional coach. At the age of seventy-five, Shrubb was reinstated as an amateur by the AAA!

The Irish had always been prominent in the early years of field events and in 1881, one family had enjoyed a virtual monopoly. Patrick Davin, a solicitor from Carrick-on-Suir, set AAA Championship records for the high jump (6ft 0.5in/1.84 metres) and the long jump (22ft 11in/6.98 metres), while his brother, Maurice, won the shot (39ft 6.5in/12.05 metres) and the hammer (98ft 10in/30.12 metres). At thirty-nine Maurice was the oldest man competing the Championships and we should remember that his hammer had a wooden shaft. Patrick, too, enjoyed none of the refinements of a later age and he jumped from grass on to grass. It was the start of a great Irish tradition and from that year until 1912, eighty-five championships were taken by Irishmen. Their names became legendary at the time. Dr William 'Jumbo' Barry won seven titles in hammer and shot, taking his last in 1895 at the age of thirty-two; Tom Keily won his fifth hammer title in 1902; and James Mitchel took five titles in the hammer and the shot between 1886-8.

But there were two men outstanding out of an already fine body of Irish athletes — Denis Horgan and Peter O'Connor. Horgan won the shot a record thirteen times between 1893 and 1913, including seven Championships in succession 1893-9. A seventeen-stone giant of a man who trained on a concoction of one dozen eggs mixed into a pint of sherry, Horgan was, as you might expect, the subject of a wealth of stories. In 1900 he lost his shot title to America's Richard Sheldon who went on to become the Olympic champion in Paris that month. Not to be outdone, Horgan worked his passage to the United States to bid for the American title. He arrived at Manhatten Field just in time for the event and it was a complete surprise to Sheldon when Horgan was announced. It was a superb piece of psychological warfare and Sheldon watched dumbfounded as Horgan stepped forward to heave the shot 46ft 1.75in (14.06 metres) and gain his revenge. Horgan went on winning AAA titles — and an Olympic silver medal — long after having a steel plate inserted into his skull after some New York Italians attacked him with a shovel during a subsequent visit to that city when he found temporary employment as a policeman.

Peter O'Connor was another great Irish character of the early days of athletics as we know the sport. O'Connor, like most of his kind, doubled at both high jump and long jump, winning the AAA high jump twice and the long jump six times — in consecutive years from 1901-6. O'Connor held the Championship long jump record of 23ft 9.5in (7.25 metres) for twenty years, and his world record of 24ft 11.75in (7.61 metres), set in Dublin in August 1901, enjoyed similar longevity and was a United Kingdom best for fifty-nine years. It was not bettered as an Irish All-Comers' record until Lynn Davies passed it in 1968 — sixty-seven years and two days later. O'Connor had a devastatingly simple technique. He went 'for all I'm worth' and then, about four paces from the take-off point, he just closed his eyes 'put my trust in God' and sailed away. One suspects that O'Connor had his tongue in his cheek when he related his technique thus. Like all champions, he had the skill, ambition and courage to force himself on. Those early heroes of track and field may seem almost quaint when viewed from the late twentieth century. But let us make no mistake — they were the classic athletes of their day.

# MARATHON LOSER WHO ECLIPSED HIS CONQUEROR

'No event in the athletic history of Great Britain has aroused so much public enthusiasm' was how the London *Daily Telegraph* described the 1908 Olympiad held in that city. It went on: 'The crowning day of the great Games will be reached only next week when the "Marathon Race" will be run over a distance of 26 miles, starting from the walls of Windsor and finishing in the exhibition grounds. Twenty-two different nations are represented in an amicable contest which reminds us that by slow but sure degrees, civilisation is moving towards the friendly federation of mankind.'

These were lofty words and ideals indeed — and not a little naive when one considers the conflict between nations still to come, not least the politics inexorably bound with future Olympic Games — but nonetheless they did illustrate the immense interest in the 1908 marathon. To understand it we must go back to the first of the modern Olympiads, in Athens in 1896, when a Greek shepherd, Spyridon Louis, ran the 26 miles from the old battlefield of Marathon to Athens, arriving more than seven minutes ahead of his nearest rival. Of all the Olympic events, reborn by the French Baron de Coubertin, the marathon is the most direct link with the Games of Ancient Greece. About 500BC, Pheidippides, an Olympic champion, was first sent to enlist the help of the Spartans against the Persians who were intent on capturing Athens. After a journey of two days and nights, Pheidippides went into battle and took part in a great Greek victory on the plain of Marathon. He then returned to Athens, delivered the message, 'Rejoice, we conquer', and promptly dropped down dead in the very best traditions of the Greek epic.

Thus, the marathon embodies all the ideals of the classical Greek heroes; and it was perhaps the will of the Gods that a Greek shepherd should win the first such event in the modern Games.

The 1900 Olympic marathon, held in Paris, was won by a Frenchman, Michel Theato, and then in the 1904 Games in St Louis, the marathon produced high drama, alleged scandal, and a moment of black comedy. An American called Fred Lorz was the man at the centre of the scandal and the comedy. He had covered some nine miles when cramp gripped his aching legs in its vice-like hold and he was glad to accept a lift from a passing truck and to forget all about Olympic glory. But in those early days of the internal combustion engine, rides in such vehicles were not always destined to end in quite the right place and some five miles from the St Louis stadium where a crowd was gathered to cheer in the winner, the truck broke down and Fred Lorz was obliged to get out and complete the journey on foot so that he might be reunited with his clothes. Lorz was, of course, now refreshed and eventually trotted nimbly into the Olympic arena to the roars of his fellow countrymen who imagined that they were seeing a hero of classical Greek proportions. Lorz apparently went along with this — perhaps swept along on the tide of emotion — and it was only when the President's daughter, Alice Roosevelt, appeared to congratulate him that the truth came out. The American Athletic Union handed Lorz a life ban.

But even then the story of the 1904 marathon was not over. A British-born American, Thomas Hicks, won the race, but only after receiving considerable assistance. While Lorz was running full of vigour into the stadium, Hicks was staggering blindly along. He was given eggs, brandy, water — even a dose of strychnine — and with three 'helpers' to see to his comforts over the last few painful miles he overcame an objection to take the gold medal, finishing six minutes ahead of the second man with a time of 3hr 28min 53sec. Hicks was in terrible trouble over the last few miles and at one point his life was in the balance, as too was that of at least one other runner who inhaled abrasive dust. Hicks was only persuaded to continue after being told that Lorz had been disqualified; and Lorz, though receiving that life ban, was allowed back the following year when he won the Boston marathon.

All this, then, was the background behind the Olympic Games marathon of 1908. The Games themselves were the real forerunner of today's events, organised as a sporting festival in their own right, unlike Athens and Paris where they were part of a wider trade fair. The marathon distance was fixed at 26 miles 385 yards and this too became a standard which is maintained today. The runners included the South African Charles Hefferon, the British hopefuls, Duncan, Lord and Price, and the man who really captured the public's imagination, Tom Longboat, a Canadian Indian. There was Dorando Pietri, largely unknown, a 23-year-old confectioner from Northern Italy who began his marathon career by accident. Apparently Dorando, when seventeen-years-old, was asked to deliver a letter. Instead of posting it, he ran all the way — over thirty miles! Dorando was listed in the official runners as P. Dorando, thus ensuring that he would be forever remembered by his first name.

At just after half past two on the afternoon of 24 July 1908, HRH Princess Mary, Princess of Wales, gave the signal for the race to begin and out swept fifty-six athletes representing sixteen countries (not twenty-two as the *Daily Telegraph* had suggested). They set off at a remarkable pace under the blazing sun, out through the Sovereign's Gate of Windsor Castle and into the winding streets of the town. The British runner, Clarke, took the early lead followed by Burn and Longboat of Canada, Barnes of Great Britain and Dorando. The first mile was completed in the cracking pace of 5min 1.4sec. The first nine miles were completed in just ten seconds under an hour with Price now in the lead from Hefferon, who passed Lord for second place, and Dorando now only about four seconds behind. At Ruislip station, the halfway stage, Hefferon had cut Price's lead to

less than a minute with Price clocking 1hr 15min 13sec. Lord was still in third place ahead of Dorando. At fourteen miles Hefferon took the lead and Longboat was now closing on Dorando and Lord. The Canadian Indian came past the little Italian and drew level, whereupon the Englishman veered off the road and into the arms of a spectator, though he was to recover and finish fifth.

With Price now out of the race and Lord struggling it was Hefferon, Longboat and Dorando. Longboat's tactics were puzzling — sharp bursts of speed punctuated with rest periods — and after seventeen miles he was finished and ended the race by car, enjoying a bottle of champagne. Now Hefferon increased his lead over Dorando to 3min 13sec at the eighteen-mile mark. At nineteen miles he was a further eighteen seconds ahead. On the Harrow Road the pace quickened further with Dorando covering the mile in an astonishing 5min 58sec, dragging back the gap between the Italian and the South African by fourteen seconds. By twenty-four miles Dorando had cut the lead to less than ninety seconds. At Old Oak Common Lane, Dorando had sight of the leader. Before Hefferon had reached Wormwood Scrubs prison, the Italian, with a suicidal burst of speed, shot into the lead while the nineteen-year-old American, J.J. Hayes ran past the now-exhausted Hefferon and into second place.

Dorando was now himself thoroughly exhausted and as he entered the White City

*John Hayes, the eventual winner of the 1908 Olympic marathon, passing through Willesden. He finished behind Dorando but took the gold medal.*

*Dorando Pietri of Italy is helped over the line during the 1908 Olympic marathon, for this he was disqualified.*

Stadium to the roars of 100,000 people, he wobbled and buckled. Then the roars were stifled — Dorando, now blinded by exhaustion, had taken the wrong turn into the stadium and was running in the opposite direction. Officials called to him and he realised his mistake and turned around and wobbled back towards the tape. He went twenty yards and then collapsed, rising after perhaps thirty seconds to continue his way. Between that point and the tape Dorando fell four, perhaps five times, and was besieged with attendants, even spectators, who pulled him to his feet, massaged his legs and gave him water. He tottered through the tape ahead of the much fresher John Hayes and was unconscious before the crowd could acclaim him. The last ten yards had been a nightmare for both runner and spectators — and, of course, it had all been in vain.

Dorando had to be disqualified, of that there was no doubt. The fact that the Italian flag was raised above the Stars and Stripes may have added to the confusion, but the little confectioner from Northern Italy had received so much attention that there was never any question that he could be allowed the gold medal. Of course, race officials were left with a terrible dilemma as Dorando lay on the track in the last few yards of this gruelling race. They knew that they should not help him and that, after his incredible effort, he ought to be given the chance to finish the race unaided. But there were humane questions. Dorando looked near to death. They had to go to his aid. Indeed, for some hours after the marathon, Dorando's life hung in the balance. The Olympic Committee gave the race to Hayes with Hefferon second and two Americans in third and fourth places. Dorando, according to one report, had lost more than 10lb in bodyweight and had suffered a displaced heart which was more than half an inch out of position.

But the little Italian did have some consolation. Queen Alexandra had been so moved by his superhuman efforts that she presented him with a special cup on which was inscribed: 'For P. Dorando, In Remembrance of the Marathon Race from Windsor to the Stadium. From Queen Alexandra.' That was not all. In future marathon races, Dorando twice beat Hayes in races ending at New York's Madison Square Garden. He had also won a special place in the hearts of the British people. The 1908 Olympic marathon was one of the greatest long distance races of all time. The name of Dorando Pietri lived on, long after most people had forgotten the name of the gold medallist. For almost everyone, little Dorando was the real winner that day.

# JIM THORPE - CHAMPION WHO NEVER WAS

A glance at the Official Report of the 1912 Olympics tells the reader nothing about the feats of Jim Thorpe, part Irish, part French, part Sac and Fox Indian, whose Indian name, Wa-Tho-Huck, meant Bright Path. Yet although Jim Thorpe's name does not appear in the records of that Stockholm Olympiad, he had been told by the King of Sweden. 'You, sir, are without doubt the greatest athlete in the world.' To back up that remark the king could look back over the Games and recall that within the space of nine days, Jim Thorpe had lived up to his Indian name by burning a bright path to the gold medals in both the pentathlon and the decathlon — the first time the events had been included in the Olympic programme — and had also finished equal fourth in the high-jump and seventh in the long-jump.

The reason why Thorpe's name has been expunged from the records is quite simple: He had, it was alleged, at one time infringed the laws of amateurism. He had not done so in any dishonest way; and he had never tried to make any secret of the fact that, in 1909 and 1910, along with other college boys, he had received money for playing baseball on a minor league circuit in North Carolina. It seems so trivial, but involvement in any kind of professional sport, however far removed it may be from any Olympic event, effectively barred — and still does — participation in what is supposed to be an essentially amateur festival. The ideals may be grand — though just what constitutes 'professionalism' is a rather cloudy issue when one considers the many performers, notably from Iron Curtain countries, who appear to be amateur in name only — but it is a sad fact that Jim Thorpe, great athlete that he was, is remembered best for a misdemeanour carried out several months before he strode so magnificently across the Olympic arena.

When the American team for the 1912 Olympics was chosen, Jim Thorpe, then twenty-four years old, was a student at the Carlisle Indian School in Pennsylvania. A track and field star — as well as being an outstanding footballer — Thorpe's selection for the United States team was a formality. Towards the middle of June that year he and some 150 other sportsmen and women set sail in the *Finland* a specially chartered ship which had been extensively adapted into almost a floating gymnasium. Thorpe and his team mates landed in Stockholm on 6 July and the young part-Indian was soon in action. The following day, a Sunday, he took the field at the beginning of the pentathlon. The events were the running long jump (the standing long jump was still an event in Sweden), 200 metres, discus, javelin and 1,500 metres. It was a gruelling competition made more so by the fact that all the events were held on that one day. Eighteen competitors lined up for the long jump and initially the field was led by Avery Brundage of the United States. Brundage, later president of the International Olympic Committee and a great champion of the amateur status, jumped 6.58 metres (21ft 7.25in). That was bettered by another American, James Donahue, who managed 6.83 metres (22ft 5in), and then the Norwegian, Ferdinand Bie, went two centimetres further. Then came Jim Thorpe. He hit the board at terrific speed and went into an unassailable leap of 7.07 metres (23ft 2.5in).

The javelin part of the pentathlon saw Thorpe beaten for the only time that day when Sweden's Hugo Wieslander threw 49.56 metres (162ft 7in). After two events Thorpe was in the lead with Bie and Oscar Lemming of Sweden between him and his fellow countryman Brundage. Now all eyes turned to the track and the 200 metres which was run in nine heats with each runner being timed separately. Thorpe raced home in 22.9 seconds, a tenth of a second faster than his two nearest rivals. Bie stayed second overall behind Thorpe with Donahue now lying in third spot. The field was now down to the leading twelve competitors who now went forward to the discus.

Here again Thorpe emerged the winner, throwing the discus 35.57 metres (116ft 8.5in) to beat Brundage 34.72 metres (113ft 7in). This left just the 1,500 metres and once more Jim Thorpe stormed away. He went ahead in the second lap and took the race in 4min 44.8sec — almost five seconds ahead of another American, Menaul. Thorpe was the undisputed pentathlon champion with four victories and second place giving him six points. The second man, Bie, was well behind the American with twenty-one points. Thorpe received his gold medal, together with a bronze bust of King Gustav V, and the pentathlon champion had only just started his remarkable performance. There was still the decathlon to come.

That event began on 13 July and, because of the number of entries, continued over until the third day. The points system for the decathlon was different from that of the pentathlon. In the five-event competition points had been allocated according to placings; in the ten-event competition points were awarded on a sliding scale based on the

Jim Thorpe - the man who was told by the King of Sweden that he was the greatest athlete in the world but who was stripped of his Olympic titles.

record for the 1908 Games with 1,000 points for equalling the record and adjusted up or down as necessary. The first day saw three events and in the first of these — the 100 metres — ten heats were run with three men in each. Thorpe clocked 11.2 seconds against 11.00 seconds from Eugene Mercer and Sweden's Jacobsson. They received 952.4 points; Thorpe was awarded 904.80. After an hour's rest the competitors came back into the searing heat of the stadium for the running long jump. Despite winning this event in the pentathlon, Thorpe managed only 6.79 metres (22ft 3.5in). The Swede, Lomberg, topped them all with 6.87 metres (22ft 6.5in). Thorpe was now second overall with 1,735.75 points behind Mercer with 1,795.60. The final event of the day was the shot and here Thorpe took the lead. He put 12.89 metres (42ft 3.5in), six centimetres better than Einar Nilsson.

The following morning the first event of the day was the running high jump which Thorpe took with consumate ease, clearing 1.87 metres (6ft 1.5in) while George Philbrook, an American, and Lomberg each cleared 1.75 metres (5ft 8.75in). The positions in the overall competition were changing below Thorpe but the part-Indian hero still maintained the lead. Now came the 400 metres when the field had been whittled down to eighteen with six heats of three runners each. Thorpe was beaten into second place in his heat, one tenth of a second behind the Canadian, Lukeman, while Mercer topped the event with 49.9 seconds. The overall positions now read: Thorpe 4,359.87 points; Lomberg 3,911.39; Mercer 3,885.20.

In the discus Thorpe finished third behind Philbrook, who became the only athlete in the decathlon to pass the 1,000-points standard, and Schaeffer. The distances were: Philbrook 41.56 metres (136ft 4in), Schaeffer 37.14 (121ft 10in), Thorpe 36.98 metres (121ft 4in). Philbrook's great effort leapfrogged him up to second place in the overall table and now the athletes set themselves ready for the 110 metres hurdles. Again there were six heats of three men each and Thorpe won his heat with the very good time of 15.6 seconds. No other decathlete could get past 16.2 seconds and Thorpe ended the second day with 6,132.63 points, well ahead of Philbrook (5,553.82), Lomberg (5,432.21) and Wieslander (5,425.32).

The final day began with the pole vault and Mercer, a specialist at this event, won easily with a leap of 3.60 metres (11ft 9.75in). This took him to fourth in the overall table behind Thorpe, Lomberg and Wieslander while Philbrook could not even clear the zero standard and slipped right back. Wieslander took the javelin, as expected, but with Thorpe throwing fourth-best, the student from Carlisle Indian School had only to finish the 1,500 metres to be sure of his second gold medal. The race was again in heats and after Holmer won the first, and Kugelberg the second, Jim Thorpe stormed home in his heat with remorseless efficiency.

Thus Thorpe took another gold medal. He tallied an amazing 8,412 points out of a possible 10,000 with an overall lead over the silver medallist Wieslander of 688 points. Thorpe was 999 points ahead of Lomberg — all but the standard for one event — and now he was hailed as the greatest athlete in the world. Thorpe, who also picked up a silver model of a viking longboat, rejected £100 to run at a meeting in Scotland and returned home with little more than the clothes in which he stood, plus, of course, his bronze and silver prizes which added to two gold medals. On his return Thorpe was inundated with offers to turn professional but rejected them all, 'not wishing to make money out of his athletic skills'. He continued to compete as a highly-successful amateur, beating the Olympic champion, Frederick Kelly, over 110 metres hurdles in a time of 15 seconds which equalled the world record, though it was never ratified. In September he took the all-round championship of the American Athletic Union and looked set for another great season. Then the storm broke. Early in 1913 the AAU 'convicted' Jim Thorpe of professionalism. He was to return all his Olympic trophies, his records would be deleted and his points deducted.

The rest of the sporting world was staggered. There were now new gold, silver and bronze medallists of the 1912 Olympic Games six months after they had ended. It was as if Jim Thorpe had never existed. What made the matter even more shocking was that Thorpe had earned a few dollars in minor baseball — a sport which had nothing at all to do with the AAU — and he had refused lucrative offers to capitalise on his athletic prowess. Thorpe did recover however. A week later he signed for New York Giants baseball club. After World War I he became a professional football star with Ganton Bulldogs, having played baseball for Boston Braves in 1919. After 1926 Thorpe retired from major football and when the Olympic Games were held in Los Angeles in 1932 he was unable to afford a ticket. He died alone, in a trailer camp in California, in 1953, three years after being voted the greatest American sportsman of the first half of the twentieth century. Yet as far as the Olympic Games officials are concerned, Jim Thorpe, double gold medal winner, was the champion who never was.

# THE FLYING FINNS

The 1920 Olympic Games held in Antwerp saw the Olympic oath uttered for the first time together with the unfurling, also for the first time, of the Olympic flag. The Games also saw the Olympic debut of a stocky, poker-faced middle and long distance runner from Finland called Paavo Nurmi. Nurmi was hardly known outside his native land but in these Games he took three gold medals — in the 10,000 metres and the cross country (individual and team) — and a silver in the 5,000 metres. With further gold medals in the marathon, shot, discus, pentathlon and decathlon, and the triple jump, Finland were the outstanding nation in the 1920 Olympic athletics.

When the 1924 Games came round, held in Paris by French officials who were determined there would be no repeat of the 1900 Olympic shambles in that same city, Paavo Nurmi was still there, together with another strong Finnish contingent. On the eve of the Games a Finnish official declared, 'We have reduced our athletics to a science . . . you shall see.' It was no empty boast. Nurmi's career had really begun in Antwerp four years earlier. Now he went into these latest Olympics with a string of broken world records behind him. He had eclipsed the barriers in the mile, 1,500 metres, 2,000 metres, 3,000 metres, three miles, 5,000 metres, 10,000 metres and 15,000 metres. It was an incredible record for one man and in addition to Nurmi, Finland also had Ville Ritola who had just returned from America to clip nearly five seconds off Nurmi's 10,000 metres record. The first day of the athletics events in the 1924 Games belonged to Finland. Though a crowd of over 50,000 groaned with disappointment when they learned that Nurmi would not be taking part in the 10,000 metres that day, they were more than compensated by the performance of Ritola. He took the gold with ease, clocking 30min 23.2sec to trim 12.2 seconds off his own world record and finish more than twenty seconds ahead of the silver medallist, Edvin Wide of Sweden. With Finns Eero Berg and Vaino Sipila in third and fourth places, and Jonni Myyra retaining his javelin gold Finland had opened their Games with a bang.

The following day saw Ritola win his heat in the 3,000 metres steeplechase while in the other heats of that event Elias Katz set a new Olympic record of 9min 43.8sec. With Ebb finishing third in his heat, Finland now had three men in the final. When Eero Lehtonen retained his pentathlon title Finland had three gold medals — and Paavo Nurmi had still not appeared on the scene! Nurmi's first appearance was in the heats of the 5,000 metres. After Finland's Rastas had won the first heat, Nurmi came out, nestling a stopwatch in his right palm. The gun went and Nurmi gathered up his easy, flowing rhythm and though he was happy to let the Indian runner Singh take an early lead, when Nurmi's moment came he simply slipped into top gear and coasted home in 15min 28.6sec. It was a minute outside his own world record, set a month previously, but the crowd had come simply to see him run. With Seppala third in that heat, and Ritola third in his heat, the Finns had four men in the twelve-man final two days hence.

The following day Ritola won his second gold medal of the Games with victory in the 3,000 metres steeplechase. Nurmi, meanwhile, was in the heats of the 1,500 metres. Again he carried his stop-watch; again he executed a clinical performance; and again Finland had four men in a twelve-man final. In the 3,000 metres steeplechase Katz took the silver medal — after seeing Ritola take more than ten seconds off his two-day old record — and Finland might have had the bronze as well, had not Ebb run out of steam on the last lap. Ritola, incidentally, had bested the previous world record as well as the Olympic barrier. Though these Games

*The legendary Flying Finn, Paavo Nurmi.*

are remembered most of all for the performances of Nurmi, Ritola was setting an amazing standard of consistency.

The Thursday dawned — 10 July 1924 — and now Nurmi was set to etch his name indelibly on the history of the Olympic Games. He was about to become a legend, the man who would perform a double winning run which would be unique in the history of athletics. Nurmi's first challenge was the final of the 1,500 metres. He came out on to the red shale track of the Colombes Stadium just before a quarter to three that afternoon and a cursory glance at the field told him that the gold medal was his for the taking. His only serious challenger, the Briton Hyla Stallard, was there after an exceptionally good time in the heats, but with an ankle now heavily bandaged after a fall. Nurmi almost trotted round the track, even giving up his stop-watch at the start of the second lap, and coasted home in 3min 53.6 sec — just one

second outside his world record. For Paavo Nurmi the acquisition of another Olympic gold medal had seemed to require no more effort from him than that needed to undertake a pleasant training run.

One hour later, Nurmi was lining up for the final of the 5,000 metres. This time he had his watch with him and did not let it go. For the first half of the race it appeared as though his opponents were intent on burning out the Finn. Yet he stayed with them and one by one they dropped back until Nurmi glanced once more at his watch to make sure that he was on schedule. The last lap found Ritola on the heels of his countryman, but unable to draw level. Several times Ritola looked likely to bother Nurmi; each time the champion drove harder and he passed the tape in 14min 31.2 sec, three seconds outside his own world record but well inside the Olympic record set up by Kolehmainen in 1912. The Swede, Wide, fought off the challenge of Rastas and Seppala to finish with the bronze, albeit over 200 yards behind the Finnish gold and silver medallists.

On Friday, Nurmi, Ritola and Tala took Finland through to the final of the 3,000 metres team race, an event now discontinued, and on Saturday another event now dropped from the Olympic Games, the 10,000 metres cross-country, was staged. Nurmi had won this event in Antwerp and he was favourite here, though the near-90°F temperature favoured no one at all. The athletes paraded in the stadium and then the race was started outside the arena. When it was announced that the leaders were back and making for the track, the excitement grew almost to pandamonium. In fact there was only one leader. As all the others faltered or fell by the wayside in the searing heat, Paavo Nurmi trotted into the Colombes stadium apparently untroubled by the scorching temperature. He won the race in 32min 54.8sec and then slowed to walking pace and calmly strode to the dressing room where many other men would have collapsed. Ritola, running his seventh race in as many days, took the silver some twenty seconds behind Nurmi. Then came America's Johnson

*Nurmi (right) edges his fellow countryman Ville Ritola out of the gold medal place in the 1924 Olympic Games 5,000 metres.*

and Great Britain's Harper. Harper collapsed on the line and that was the signal for what followed. In they came, the rest of those who had finished — only twenty out of an original thirty-nine — staggering and falling. The Spaniard, Andia Aguilar, even took the wrong turning, much as Dorando Pietri had done in 1908. He too was on the verge of death and though he survived, the 10,000 metres cross-country race did not.

On Sunday, the closing day of the Games track and field events, Nurmi and Ritola helped Finland to the gold medal in the 3,000 metres team race. Nurmi finished first, breaking the Olympic record with 8min 32sec, a time which was not far short of his world record for the distance. Now only the marathon stood between Finland and the incredible feat of having won every race from that distance right down to the 1,500 metres. Albin Stenroos, a salesman from Helsinki, had finished third in the 10,000 metres in 1912. Now aged thirty-five he attempted to complete a 'grand slam' for Finland. He did it, some six minutes ahead of the silver medallist, Romeo Bertini of Italy. Yet another Finn, Lauri Halonen, finished fourth.

These had been great days for Finnish athletics. Paavo Nurmi, winner of seven races in six days, was the one we all remember, and rightly so, for he can be called one of, perhaps *the*, greatest middle and long distance runners of all time. Yet little Ville Ritola might have worn that crown had it not been for the almost super-human feats of Nurmi. Ritola had won four gold medals, counting the team events, and two silver, in eight days. These two 'Flying Finns' continued their track battle long after these Olympics were closed. Six weeks after Paris, Nurmi took from Ritola his 10,000 metres world record; they met six times in indoor races in America, Nurmi winning five of the battles; and in the 1928 Amsterdam Olympics they fought out the 10,000 metres once again; and once again there was gold and there was silver for Finland as Ritola followed Nurmi over the finishing line. Ritola had his revenge in the 5,000 metres, winning with ease, but that effort cost him his 3,000 metres steeplechase title. The event was still won by a Finn, Toivo Loukola, while Nurmi had the silver medal. Just to underline that Finland was still a power with which to be reckoned, Harri Larva won the 1,500 metres for that country.

In 1932 Nurmi suffered a severe setback. By now he was concentrating on the marathon and planned to attack the Olympic title at Los Angeles. Alas, in April of that year the IAAF suspended him for allegedly breaking amateur regulations. He protested, but even an eve-of-the-Games petition signed by no less than seventeen marathon runners failed to sway the IAAF decision. It is a story with a happy ending, however. When Helsinki hosted the Olympic Games in 1952, the man chosen to carry the Olympic torch into the arena was...Paavo Nurmi. His step was just as light, his action just as ruthlessly efficient. The last of the Flying Finns flew gracefully once more.

# BRITANNIA RULES THE LANES

When Steve Ovett ousted his great rival Seb Coe to take the 800 metres gold medal in the 1980 Moscow Olympics, it was the first time in ten Olympiads that the title had gone to Britain. Yet in the first four Olympics after World War I, the two-lap race was an entirely British preserve as first Albert Hill (in 1920), then Douglas Lowe (1924 and 1928) and finally Tommy Hampson (1932) took the gold. Yet if these three dominated middle-distance running, there can be little point in trying to compare them in an attempt to discover exactly what was the common denominator which made them such classic performers. The truth was that no one runner was anything like the other two. Albert Hill, a veteran of warfare in France, was a broad man with long legs; Douglas Lowe was handsome and cleanly built; and Tommy Hampson stood over six feet tall and wore spectacles.

The story of Britain's dominance at this distance began in 1919 at the AAA Championships at Stamford Bridge when a thirty-year-old former Royal Flying Corps wireless operator won the 880 yards and the mile in the same afternoon. Albert Hill, who had won the AAA four miles in 1910 ran the heat and final of the 880 yards (which he won in 1min 55.2sec), the mile (in 4min 21.2sec) and the 880 yards leg of the one mile medley relay which was won by his Polytechnic Harriers. Though regarded as being past his prime, Albert Hill then set his heart on winning both the 800 metres and the 1,500 metres at the following year's Olympic Games in Antwerp. Yet before those Games began — and Britain thought long and hard before sending a team at all after war had halted the progress of the sport in the United Kingdom,

unlike the neutral countries — Hill was surprisingly beaten in the AAA Championships. He was out run by the Oxford University runner Bevil Rudd, who went on to win the 440 yards that afternoon, thus attracting the British selectors who invited the Devon-born runner to represent the country of his birth. Rudd, however, chose to run for South Africa, his father's country.

Hill had been troubled by a leg injury in the 880 yards but he overcome objections to him appearing in both events in Antwerp and duly found himself in the Belgian city still suffering from the after-effects of war. The facilities were poor, the stadium left much to be desired, and Hill would have been forgiven for thinking that the odds were stacked against him. But this 31-year-old possessed a temperament as calm as a mill-pond. Armed with that, and a great deal of information about his opponents which had been amassed by his coach, Sam Mussabini, Hill began his task. Like most things at this Olympiad, the seeding left much to be desired and Hill found himself in the same heat as Rudd and Earl Eby, the fine American runner. Hill qualified in second place behind the South African, then went through with an easy semi-final. In the 800 metres final, Eby began with a fast first lap of 54.2 seconds and with just over 300 metres to run, Rudd burst into the lead and gave himself a clear lead. Hill waited his turn and with some twenty metres to run he broke through to take the gold in 1min 53.4sec. Eby had the silver, and Rudd, who injured an ankle on the rough track, limped in for the bronze. It was an excellent performance by the Briton who had used all his knowledge of his opponents to plan out exactly when to make his break.

Two days later Albert Hill waited for the start of the 1,500 metres final. His 800 metres winning time was a British record; now the Polytechnic Harrier wanted to add the 1,500 metres to his list of honours. The weather was dreadful. Rain was falling heavily and the track was about as firm as the mud of Flanders two years earlier. Hill and Philip Noel-Baker (later Lord Noel-Baker, Nobel

*Tommy Hampson on the victory stand after winning the 800 metres event in the Olympic Games, 1932*

Games, for Albert Hill's double was an epic achievement. Hill had one more great race to run. His ambition was to beat the world mile record set by the American Norman Taber with 4min 12.6sec in 1915. In 1922, at the AAA Championships, Hill decided to have a crack at that record, even though he was now 32 years old. He ran the first lap in 59.6 seconds and at the half-mile had clocked 2min 4sec. One by one the twenty other runners had been picked off. All except twenty-year-old Hyla Stallard, the Oxford and Cambridge champion, who refused to give up. At the bell, reached in 3min 11.2sec, Stallard was still there and closing hard. But Hill was too wily for the youngster. The old fox had run the third lap in a comfortable time and now he had plenty in reserve. The final lap came in 62.6 seconds and Hill was home in 4min 13.8sec. It was outside the world record, but clipped a full three seconds off the British record first set by Joe Binks in the 1902 AAA Championships. It was another classic run by Albert Hill. The great Sydney Wooderson could have had no better coach when Hill took him over.

The next great British Olympic 800 metres runner was Douglas Lowe, born in Manchester and educated at Highgate School before he went up to Cambridge. Yet it was not to Lowe that Britain looked for success in the 1924 Paris Olympics, but Stallard and his partner, Edgar Mountain. When Hill won the AAA mile in 1921, Mountain won the 880 yards (and had finished fourth in the Olympics 800 metres the previous year). In 1922, Mountain was again first in the AAA 880 yards and Stallard second in the mile; in 1923 it was Stallard who won the mile and Mountain who finished second in the half-mile; and in 1924, Stallard won the 880 yards with Lowe less than a yard behind him.

But though Lowe had been outshadowed in the build-up to the Games, it was to him that Britain turned. First, Mountain tripped in the semi-final and was eliminated; then the effort of having to set the early pace finally told on Stallard in the final. Stallard took the field through the first 700 metres but then flagged and it was the 21-year-old

Peace Prize winner of 1959) were the British favourites. It was Noel-Baker, veteran of the 1912 Games, who took the lead for the first three laps; at the bell, Hill took over and went through for the gold in 4min 1.8sec, with his team captain taking the silver.

There can have been fewer more impressive performances by a Briton in the Olympic

25

Lowe who became an Olympic champion in 1min 52.4sec. These were unhappy times for Stallard. In the 1,500 metres heat he suffered a stress fracture to a bone in his right foot and then ruptured a ligament. He still managed the bronze medal, however, tumbling over the line just ahead of Lowe.

Lowe was a hero at Olympic level, yet he had still not won an AAA title and in 1925 it was Cecil Griffiths who took the 880 yards and Bernard McDonald the mile. But the following year, Douglas Lowe did achieve a classic performance. The AAA lifted its ban on German competitors imposed in 1918 and this opened the door for Dr Otto Peltzer, the German 400 metres, 1,500 metres and 400 metres hurdles champion. Well over 25,000 people were in Stamford Bridge to see Lowe set a blistering pace. He covered the first lap in 54.6 seconds that afternoon, then saw the German, apparently beaten, come back to scorch through the tape in 1min 51.6sec to get well inside the world record of 1min 52.2sec set by Ted Meredith. Lowe had lost, but he too was well inside the old record, though he was untimed, and he had now shown his best form on a British track at last.

Again, Lowe had failed to win an AAA Championship. But in 1927 he more than made up for his earlier disappointments, winning both the 440 yards and 880 yards — and then repeating that double in the Olympic year which followed. Lowe was thus well fortified when he went to the Amsterdam Games. He went through sweetly to the 800 metres final once more, this time to face the American title holder, Lloyd Hahn, and the world record-holder over that distance, Sera Martin of France. From the gun, Lowe moved into the lead and reached the bell in 55.2 seconds, just behind Hahn, who he had allowed to assume the lead. At the last turn, Lowe struck. He ran a devastating home stretch to finish a full second ahead of Bylehn, the Swede. it was a new Olympic record of 1min 51.8sec. Now Lowe had just one score to settle. Otto Peltzer had been injured and was eliminated in the semi-finals of the 800 metres in Amsterdam. In August that year, with the German now fully fit, they met in Berlin. Lowe ran his personal best of 1min 51.2sec, beating the German into the bargain. Peltzer was a full second behind Lowe who, having made his point, retired.

The stage of English middle-distance running was not empty for long. Tommy Hampson, born in London in October 1907, beat Lowe's English native record for 880 yards when he clocked 1min 53.2sec in 1930. Amazingly, this was Hampson's AAA debut and in beating the record he also beat the world record-holder, Sera Martin, and Cyril Ellis, winner of the AAA mile for the three previous years. Hampson was not a particularly outstanding athlete at the onset of his career, yet he had the happy knack of running his best races on the day it mattered most. In 1930 he went to Canada and became the first British Empire champion at 880 yards, and in 1932 he went to Los Angeles, confident of winning the 800 metres gold medal for Britain.

He went as AAA champion in 1930-31 and 1932 — and 440 yards runner-up in the latter year — and planned to win the gold with two laps of 55 seconds each, which would give him a world record in an Olympic final. The Canadian Phil Edwards took the lead in the final, covering the first 200 metres in 24.4 seconds, the first lap in 52.3 seconds. At the bell, Tommy Hampson was fifteen metres behind but, having clocked 54.8 seconds, was within his schedule. Now Hampson strove for the lead and gradually regained the lost metres. He drew level with Edwards with 200 metres to go and was then forced to fight it out with another Canadian, Alex Wilson. Off the final bend Wilson moved into the lead, but Hampson would not yield. Neck and neck the two men went for the tape with first one and then the other appearing to go in front. At the tape it was Tommy Hampson in a new world record of 1min 49.7 seconds, the first man in the world to run 800 metres in under 1min 50sec. Tommy Hampson was the last of three classic middle-distance runners which Britain produced between the wars. Their like would not be seen again until almost half a century later.

# BABE DIDRIKSON - THE DALLAS CYCLONE

'I came out here to beat everybody in sight and that is exactly what I am going to do. Sure I can do anything.' The words were not uttered by some heavyweight boxer wishing to emulate the mouthings of Muhammad Ali, nor by some macho athlete waging a psychological war of words on his fellow competitors. They came instead from the mouth of an eighteen-year-old blonde who weighed just eight stones and who stood just about medium height, a good-looking girl whose only non-feminine attributes were extremely well developed arm and leg muscles. She was Mildred Didrikson, born of Norwegian parents, who lived in Port Arthur, Texas. She was speaking on the eve of the 1932 Olympic Games in Los Angeles where she was about to be crowned the greatest woman athlete that the world had ever seen.

The 1932 Olympics were only the second where women's track and field events had been allowed. Four years earlier, in Amsterdam, women had, for the first time, contested the 100 metres, 800 metres, 4 x 100 metres relay, the high jump and the discus. True, women had competed in the Olympics before — at golf and tennis in 1900 and in the swimming pool in 1912 — but women's athletics were only just being recognised. For the 1932 Games there was an extra event for the females. The javelin was included for the first time and although the 80 metres hurdles was also introduced, it was only included at the expense of the 800 metres, so the ladies had only one extra event overall. The 800 metres, incidentally, was not to be included in the women's programme again until 1960 in Rome.

These were the events then that Mildred Didrikson, known to everyone as Babe, had her sights firmly set upon, though Olympic rules restricted her to a choice of just three. She came to Los Angeles with an already phenomenal reputation behind her. During the Olympic trials at Evanstown, Illinois, in July 1932, Babe had won the women's American Athletic Union National Track and Field Championships for her club, Employers Casualty Company, practically single-handed — after that she became known as the 'one-woman track team'. In the space of two and a half hours, Babe Didrikson took part in eight events and took thirty points with five firsts, one first equal, and a fourth place. For good measure she also set two new world records.

Babe's more ordinary victories came in the 80 metres hurdles which she claimed in 12.1 seconds, the shot (39ft 6.25in), the long jump (17ft 6.625in) and the baseball throw. Babe had once managed 313 ft from centrefield to the plate; here at Evanstown, a throw of 272ft 2in was enough to leave her well clear of the rest of the field. Her world records came in the javelin — where she beat her own previous world record by a good six feet — and in the high jump where she shared her record with Jean Shiley. The Olympic trials were a formality for the girl from Texas. She was assured of a place in the American team for she was already accepted as the greatest woman athlete that this great nation had ever produced. Towards the end of July she and her women team mates — the team was sixteen-strong — booked into a Los Angeles hotel during the final build-up to the Games. For the first time an Olympic Village had been erected, but this was a totally male preserve and while it was hailed as a great success by the men who lived there for the duration of the Games, the women had to make do with rather less homely hotel accommodation.

The Games should have been officially declared open by the President of the United States, Herbert Hoover, but he was too busy worrying about the impending election in which he was being challenged by Franklin D. Roosevelt. History records that Hoover lost his own special race, that for the White

27

*'Babe' Didrikson, the Dallas Cyclone who went to the 1932 Olympic Games in Los Angeles determined 'to beat everyone out of sight'.*

Tilly Fleischer had the bronze and Japan's Masako Shimpo beat Nan Gindele into fourth place.

On 3 August, Babe lined up for the heats of the 80 metres hurdles. The times here are the significant factor. The world best at this event was 12.2 seconds accomplished by Sychrova of Czechoslovakia in 1928 and equalled by the South African, Marjorie Clarke, two years later. Babe ran in the first heat and at the halfway mark looked a little too relaxed for the comfort of her team mates. She may have sensed this for she simply quickened her pace and was home four-tenths of a second inside the world best. The second heat was won in 12.2 seconds and all these times pointed to yet another Didrikson gold medal. The logic proved accurate. The following afternoon Babe lowered the time still further. Another American, Evelyn Hall, ran her close, but the girl of Norwegian extraction went through the tape in 11.7 seconds. Hall took the silver but Marjorie Clarke upset a clean sweep for the Americans when she pushed Simone Schaller into fourth place, taking the bronze for South Africa.

Babe Didrikson had been allowed to compete in only three events and she had already claimed two gold medals. The last event was the high jump, held on 7 August, the final day for track and field events. Her old adversary, Jean Shiley, was the main threat to a hat trick of gold medals by the Dallas Cyclone. The two girls did not yield an inch against each other as the bar was upped and upped. Each kept in contention until the bar stood at 5ft 5.75in. Babe went first and clipped the bar; could Jean Shiley get over this height and take the gold medal for herself? She could not and the bar came down to 5ft 5.25in. This time both girls cleared it easily and the judges were now faced with a dilemma. They solved it in a controversial and most extraordinary way. They invoked a rule which said that a high jumper could not 'dive' over the bar. Jean Shiley had taken the bar with a scissors technique; Mildred Didrikson had employed a 'western roll' and that said the judges constituted a dive.

House, and Roosevelt gained a crushing victory. Against this background it was Charles Curtis, the vice-president, who formerly declared the Los Angeles Olympiad open on 30 July 1932. Babe Didrikson did not have long to wait before she was involved in the action. The pomp and ceremony over, the Dallas Cyclone woke up on the last day of July and mentally prepared herself for the tasks that lay ahead. Her first event was the javelin that day. The sun was still burning down on to the stadium as she came out to the acclaim of some 58,000 people — just over half the stadium capacity — at just after five o'clock that afternoon. Babe's opponents that day included a fellow American, Nan Gindele, who had, in June that year, thrown the javelin 46.74 metres (153ft 4.75in) to establish a new world best. There were also two big German girls, Tilly Fleischer, who would win a gold medal in Berlin four years later, and Ellen Braumüller, the woman whose world best had been beaten by Babe two years earlier. None of these opponents daunted the attractive blonde. Her throw took her four feet past her own world best set at Evanstown two weeks previously. Her throw was measured at 43.70 metres (143ft 4in) and there was nothing that any of the other girls could do to come anywhere near it. Ellen Braümuller took the silver medal.

It was an amazing ruling. If Didrikson's last jump was illegal then so were all her other attempts and the competition should have been stopped there and then. It seemed that the judges had only turned to this rule to disentangle themselves from a sticky situation. To make matters even more ludicrous they then awarded Babe the silver medal! Her only consolation was that she was allowed to keep her share of a new world record. Before the Games started, Babe had been asked by an American reporter to comment on just how many records she thought she might break in the Olympic stadium. She replied, with not a little bitterness, 'I'd break them all if they'd let me.' She was obviously angry that the rules had forbidden her to go for more than three events.

Babe Didrikson's problems did not end with partial disqualification in the 1932 Olympic high jump. Her fame spread and soon she was inundated with offers to turn professional, even with offers from Hollywood. In December that year, after being voted America's most outstanding woman athlete of the year, her picture and an interview appeared in a cigarette advertisement. She protested that it had been done without her knowledge, but the authorities suspended her. She announced she would take up long distance swimming and the Southern District of the AAU lifted her suspension. A year later she was banned again after announcing that she was going to turn professional. She then joined a vaudeville act, travelling through the United States 'doing the things I know how to do — putting the shot, acrobatics and playing the mouth organ'. She then turned her thoughts to golf, played exhibition matches with Gene Sarazen, and was then reinstated as an amateur, married a twenty-stone wrestler known as 'The Crying Greek from Cripple Creek', went on to win the US Amateur championship and eventually turned professional again. In 1950 Babe Zaharias, as she now was, was voted the greatest female athlete of the first half of the century. No doubt she did not argue with that assessment.

# JACK LOVELOCK WINS THE MILE OF THE CENTURY

The title 'Mile of the Century' may have been a misnomer for the race over that distance held at the Palmer Stadium track at the famous American university town of Princeton before World War II, because the race was staged annually from 1935 until the outbreak of war. Yet if the title of the event was perhaps a little too ambitious, there can be no doubt that some of the finest of all mile races held between the wars were seen at this stadium. Apart from Sydney Wooderson's failure in the event just a year before the war, the most famous of all these races was in the inaugural year when Jack Lovelock, a brilliant New Zealander, demonstrated his superiority over two of the most outstanding American runners of the 1930s.

Jack Lovelock burst upon the British athletics scene in 1932 when, as a nineteen-year-old Oxford University Freshman, he set a new British record for the mile with 4min 12sec. The following year he was selected for the combined Oxford and Cambridge Universities team which toured the United States with matches against Havard and Yale, and against Princeton and Cornell. It was in the latter match that Lovelock underlined his rapid improvement in the most emphatic manner. He smashed the world record for the mile — previously held by the Frenchman Jules Ladoumegue — with a time of 4min 7.6sec. It was a great race with Bill Bonthron, who Lovelock was meeting for the first time, pushing the New Zealander all the way. Only in the final few yards did Lovelock pull away and he sped past the tape seven yards ahead of Bonthron who had the consolation of breaking the American record for the mile.

This race captured the imagination of the American public but they had seen their last glimpse of Lovelock for some time. The New Zealander returned to England to continue his medical studies at Oxford and another American, Glenn Cunningham, eclipsed the mile record with a time of 4min 6.8sec. The American promoters were keen to stage their 'greatest' mile and a year after Lovelock's victory they asked him back to the United States. He refused, feeling unable to spare time from his medical studies. There was, however, the prospect of the New Zealander meeting one of his American challengers when a Princeton and Cornell team visited Europe. Lovelock raced against Bonthron twice, in Amsterdam and at the White City, and won both races.

In 1935, the Americans renewed their

*Jack Lovelock, the brilliant New Zealander who demonstrated his superiority over two of America's greatest runners of the inter-war period.*

invitation for Jack Lovelock to visit them for the 'Mile of the Century'. This time he felt able to accept and on 5 June 1935 Lovelock arrived in New York. He was met with disappointing news. His old rival, Bonthron, had suffered a leg ligament strain and there was doubt about his fitness. Lovelock, meanwhile, had spent his last few weeks prior to sailing across the Atlantic by arranging a series of races designed to bring himself to peak fitness for the projected epic at Princeton. Ten days after Lovelock's arrival he found himself in the locker room at Palmer Stadium, keyed up for the race. To his delight — and to the delight of the promoters — Bonthron had declared himself fit. With Cunningham also in the field, the American newspapers speculated on a mile run in 4min 5sec, or even what would then have been an incredible 4min 4sec. The Palmer Stadium track was shaped like a horseshoe and with cinders laid on top of concrete was one of the most conducive to fast times in the world. In an interview before the race Bonthron told a newspaper reporter, 'If anyone can do a mile in 4min 5sec or less, it is Jack Lovelock. He has the most springy and lively stride of any of the great milers I have run against. He runs without effort and exerts himself far less than either Cunningham or myself.' Whether Bonthron's comments were designed to wage some kind of psychological war against the New Zealander is open to conjecture, but whatever the reason they were accurate remarks.

It appeared that all America and his wife wanted to see this confrontation, a race between the best men in the world at this distance. Princeton was crowded with people who had travelled in by every possible means — train, bus, car, aeroplane, even horseback — and a day before the race there was no hotel accommodation to be had. Princeton was unused to so many visitors and many thousands slept with only the sky over their heads that night. That morning dawned fine and the crowds wound their way to Palmer Stadium, arriving early to select the best vantage points from which to see a struggle which promised to be of

Titanic proportions. The sun was slowly sinking when the six runners came out on to the track and some 40,000 people craned their necks to catch a glimpse of curly-haired Jack Lovelock.

His rivals were Bill Bonthron, formerly of Princeton University, a New York accountant and holder of the world 1,500 metres record — the 'metric mile'; Glenn Cunningham, world record miler and a Kansas City University runner; Gene Venske, from Oklahoma's Tulsa University, holder of the world indoor mile record; Joe Mangan, of New York Athletic Club, holder of the world record for the three-quarter mile and obviously included in this field to set a fast pace; and Glenn Dawson who had leaped to prominence after beating Cunningham. It was certainly a field which looked capable of producing a record time. Cunningham started the race as the favourite while Bonthron, despite his recent injury, was also expected to challenge hard, especially since this was a track which he had known intimately since boyhood. After recovering from the ligament strain Bonthron had continued the series of races which he had designed specially for an assault on the world mile record in this Princeton event.

It was anticipated that Mangan would take up the lead and set the early pace, which he did, and for the first lap, Lovelock, who hated to make his own pace, was happy to settle in at fourth position. Towards the end of that lap the New Zealander moved up to third place while Mangan, now tiring after his very fast start, dropped right back and was overtaken by Cunningham. The six runners went into the second lap and it was now obvious that the winner would come from the Cunningham-Lovelock-Bonthron trio, although as they passed the post in that order it was also obvious that there was to be no world record for they had taken 64.9 seconds to cover the first 440 yards. The second lap saw the trio draw further ahead of the rest of the field and no change in the order was made as they went round a second time in a little over one minute.

The time at the halfway stage was 2min

5.7sec and with Cunningham, Lovelock and Bonthron running so close together, there could have been hardly a yard separating them. The third lap was completed giving the time for the three-quarter mark as 3min 8.9sec. The crowd now sensed that they were seeing a great race. Each of the three front-runners had settled down nicely, each waiting for his opportunity to present itself. Lovelock, in particular, looked extremely happy, running well within himself and with as smooth an action as it is possible to achieve. Now, with 440 yards remaining, someone had to make up their mind to go. Lovelock still seemed content to stay close on Cunningham's heels, content to win the race by superior tactics, not caring for a world record. As the runners went around the first bend of this final lap, Bonthron appeared to fade. It was now becoming a two-man race as Cunningham and Lovelock prepared to fight out the last few dozen yards.

As the two men reached the final bend Lovelock made his move. In a yard he was past Cunningham and sprinting for the tape. The American looked for that final ounce of energy, that extra spurt that would bring him back into the race. He could not find it. Despite the demise of their two American hopes, the crowd now roared the Kiwi Lovelock home. Lovelock hit the tape at 4min 11.2sec, well outside the world record, but still the winner of an epic race. Bonthron, meanwhile, had summoned up a last gaspful of stamina and passed the now finished Cunningham to move past the tape in second place. He was still a good ten yards behind Lovelock with Venske fourth, thirty yards

*Lovelock (right) with one of his great US rivals, Glenn Cunningham.*

behind Cunningham with Dawson fifth, a further twelve yards out.

Lovelock walked around the track, acknowledging the cheers and applause. He looked fresh, almost as if he was about to take part in another mile race. A special dais had been erected and Lovelock took the highest point with Bonthron and Cunningham to his left and right for the benefit of photographers. The American newspapers were full of praise for the New Zealander. The *New York Times* wrote: 'Lovelock coasted serenely and majestically to victory. So effortless was his achievement that he left totally unanswered the question as to what he might have done had he been harder pressed.' The *New York Herald-Tribune* summed it up rather more succinctly: 'He left the great Cunningham standing still.' Certainly the 'Mile of the Century' had produced one of the greatest races in the history of that distance.

# TAN STREAK FROM OHIO STATE

There are many who feel that the Olympic Games, while attempting the admirable ideals of a great amateur sporting festival in which athletes of all creeds and colours come together in healthy competition, is nothing more than a platform for nationalistic fervour which only serves to inflame differences instead of putting them aside. Although the Olympic Games has its own oath of allegiance, its own anthem, and

▶

*German Olympic poster with overtones of the 'Master Race'.*

*The 1936 Berlin Olympics were used by the Nazis as a propaganda weapon. Adolf Hitler drives under the Brandenburg Gate where the Olympic flag and the swastika fly side by side.*
▼

exercises token 'sovereignty' over the arena for the duration, the flag waving, national anthems and medal tables which purport to show which country has 'won' the Games all make it difficult to argue against that. Each host country uses its organisational ability to outdo previous Games; and each takes great pride in the number of gold, silver and bronze medals won, as if to show that its way of life is better than all others. In many respects the Olympic Games has become a battle between East and West. It is hard to argue differently when the case is put for just one flag and one anthem — the Olympic — and for the doing away of medals 'league' tables. It is also naive to imagine that the great nations of the world will ever allow such a thing to happen.

The first time that the Olympic Games became an overtly political occasion was in 1936 when the Games were staged in Berlin at the height of Nazi hysteria in Hitler's Third Reich. When the Germans first learned that they would host the 1936 Olympiad it was five years away and Hitler had not yet obtained his unchallenged tyrannical grip on the country. The Nazis' first reaction was to call the Olympic Games an 'infamous festival dominated by Jews.' But as the Games approached, Hitler was now undisputed master and the Nazis were now totally aware that the Olympic Games afforded them a magnificent opportunity to feed the world great helpings of propaganda. No expense was spared in making these Olympic Games the most efficient and grand of all time.

As the German propaganda machinery swung into top gear, another event was taking place some 4,000 miles away in Ann Arbor, Michigan. At Ferry Field, on the afternoon of 25 May 1935, a crowd of about 10,000 Americans was watching the 'Big Ten', an inter-university athletics meeting which featured most of the top performers in that country. At just before a quarter past three on that afternoon, they saw J.C. Owens, the son of an Alabama negro cotton-picker, emerge for the 100 yards. James Cleveland Owens was known as 'Jesse' because in the soft southern drawl of his hometown that was how the initials 'J.C.' sounded. Owens had been troubled by a back injury throughout the build-up to the 'Big Ten', but that did not stop him this day. By four o'clock he had broken or equalled no less than six world records. In his own words it had been 'quite a day'.

Jesse Owens started with that 100 yards, winning in 9.4 seconds to equal the world record; within ten minutes he had the long jump world record all to himself with 8.13 metres (26ft 8.25in), six inches more than the old record; then came 20.3 seconds for the 220 yards straight run, and the same time for the 200 metres in the same run; and finally the 220 yards hurdles with 22.6 seconds — the 200 metres hurdles also falling in the same time and in the same race. It was one of the finest achievements in the history of athletics and when the American team for the 1936 Berlin Olympics was chosen, the name of Jesse Owens was probably the first one that the selectors pencilled in. Yet that fantastic day at Ferry Field is not what history most remembers about Jesse Owens. He is synonymous instead with Hitler and the 'Nazi' Olympics where fact and myth merged together to form a legend that is one of sports most enduring — a legend which, like so many, has rather less basis in what actually happened than what the scribes of that and subsequent times felt would make a good story.

The legend of Jesse Owens was inevitable. Here was a sporting event, arguably the greatest in the world, at which Adolf Hitler and his Nazi gang had predicted that their 'Master Race' of Ayrians would triumph over the 'lesser mortals' like Jews and Negroes. Here was a black athlete, already a world record holder, who was almost certainly going to smash Hitler's theories — and smash them on a world stage. The legend is that Owens crushed the Nazi philosophy and that Hitler, enraged by the sight of a black athlete racing and jumping to four gold medals, refused to shake his hand, instead storming from the stadium, probably to go and chew a carpet in the Reichstag.

To explain the rise of this legend we must first look at the very nature of the Olympic Games. Though, as we have already noted, each host country — and each competing country — uses the Olympics to wave its own national flag, the essence of the Games is the Olympic flag, oath and sovereignty. While the Games are in progress, the venues 'belong' to the Olympic movement. The fact that they are in America, Germany, Britain, or anywhere else for that matter, is purely incidental, in theory at least. On the first day of the 1936 Olympics, in the very first event, a German, Hans Wöllke, won the gold medal in the shot. Never before in the Olympic Games had a German male athlete taken a track or field gold. To excite Nazi fervour even more, the bronze medal in the shot also went to a German, Gerhard Stock, who finished behind the Finn, Sulo Barlund. The great American world record holder, Jack Torrance, was beaten out of sight and Adolf Hitler insisted that the two Germans should come, immediately after the medals ceremony, to the Führer's box to receive his personal congratulations. Such a thing was without precedent and the International Olympic Committee can hardly have been pleased that a national leader should take it upon himself to call up athletes in this way. Nevertheless, Hitler was overjoyed and he repeated the performance after the next two events when three Finns took a clean-sweep

of the 10,000 metres, and when Tilly Fleischer, German silver medallist in the 1932 javelin event, took the gold with another German, Luise Kruger, ending in the silver medal position.

So far all the gold medal winners had been Ayrians, but late on that first afternoon of the 1936 Olympics, an American Negro, Cornelius Johnson, took the gold in the high jump with another black American, Dave Albritton, winning the silver. This time Hitler's seat was empty. No one has ever been sure at what point the German leader left the stadium. At the time it was claimed that he left immediately before the medals ceremony; later accounts suggest, probably more accurately, that he departed just as soon as the last German high jumper was eliminated. The IOC were angry. The president, Count Henri de Baillet Latour, told Hitler that he was not to congratulate medal winners in public, especially if he was going to discriminate between Ayrian and non-Ayrian victors. Hitler replied that, as a loyal and patriotic German, he was simply overcome by the occasion and, along with thousands of other Germans, wanted to congratulate the men who had brought honour to the Fatherland. He continued to receive German athletes in private, but was not seen again shaking their hands in the official box. So, if Hitler snubbed anyone at the Berlin Olympics it was more likely the winner of the high jump, not Jesse Owens.

The official Nazi newspaper had called the Negro American athletes, 'black auxiliaries', but it was not a view held by the vast majority of the crowd, nor by the other German athletes. They were interested, first and foremost, in sport and Jesse Owens came to Berlin as a world record holder in seven events. At 5ft 10in and weighing a little over 11 stones, he was a superbly-built athlete and in the first heat of the 100 metres he equalled the Olympic record of 10.3 seconds. In the quarter-final he clocked 10.2 seconds to equal his own world record, set in

*Cornelius Johnson, winner of the high jump and the man who was first snubbed by Hitler.*

35

Chicago a month previously, but there was to be no Olympic record because wind assistance was assessed at more than two metres per second. The following day, the semi-finals and final of the 100 metres saw Owens in still meteoric form. He won the semi-final in 10.4 seconds and went forward against another American, Frank Wykoff, who had pressed him hard in their semi-final, Negro Ralph Metcalfe, Los Angeles silver medallist, Germany's Eric Borchmeyer, Lennart Strandberg (Sweden) and Martin Osendarp (Holland).

Owens was not noted for his great start, but in this race he sped away and left the rest of the field behind. He was a yard ahead of Metcalfe as he screamed through the tape in 10.3 seconds — again it was ruled that wind assistance had interfered with an Olympic record — and no words can sum Owen's race up better than those of Arthur J. Daley writing in the *New York Times:* 'Owens glided over the red clay track with the grace of a streamlined express flying over the open prairie.' If Hitler was not on hand to shake the black hand of Jesse Owens, it did not matter. Wherever he went the black athlete was feted by Germans, ordinary men and women, until the American team manager had to restrict him to the Olympic Village for fear of the over-enthusiastic fans accidentally hurting his star athlete.

Now Owens faced the great German favourite, Luz Long, in the long jump, as well as competing in the 200 metres. In the third heat of the 200 metres, Owens ran 21.2 seconds to record a new world best for that distance round a bend, clipping one-tenth of a second off the Olympic record into the bargain. That successfully negotiated, Owens then put on his track suit and went across to the long jump pit with little thought that he would fail to pass the qualifying mark of 7.15 metres (23ft 5.5in). After all, he was the world record holder. Like most athletes in

the long jump, Owens ran up for a trial attempt, not jumping, but following straight through. To his astonishment the red flag was raised — the practice run had been decreed one of his jumps and he now had only two remaining. The second run saw Owens leap well clear of the qualifying mark — but again the red flag signalled 'no jump'. The world record holder was within one jump of going out in the qualifying round. This time Luz Long came over with an encouraging word — and probably cost himself a gold medal. Owens jumped well behind the line and still managed to clear twenty-five feet with consumate ease.

The final evolved until only Owens and Long remained in contention. Each had two jumps remaining and Owens was only a fraction in front of the German who had ignored the ranting of his demonic leader and extended the hand of friendship to a fellow athlete of a different colour. Now Long pulled out all the stops and with his penultimate jump he equalled Owens's best attempt of 7.87 metres (25ft 9.75in). Owens had already beaten the Olympic record and now the German shared it with him. The roar which had greeted the German's effort now subsided into a breathless hush as the American pounded along the approach. His run began so casually and then wound itself up into machine-like efficiency before hitting the board and soaring away from the 26ft mark for the first time in Olympic history.

*Luz Long (left) and Jesse Owens. The German encouraged Owens to go for gold in the long jump and probably cost himself the title with a gesture which transcended the sinister political over-tones of the Games.*

*The Tan Streak from Ohio State. Jesse Owens graceful, streamlined sprinting style captured the hearts of the German crowd.*

Owens's jump was 7.94 metres (26ft 0.5in) and Long now faced the most incredible pressure. The gold medal was already as good as around Jesse Owens's neck and the German would have to pull out a magnificent effort, the greatest of his life, if he was to wrest it from the American. The cries of encouragement as Long hurtled along the approach groaned downwards in depair as the red flag was raised. Long had fouled the board and Owens had his second gold medal. With no pressure now on him, Owens also had one jump remaining and he used it to sail serenely to 8.06 metres (26ft 5.25in). It was to remain an Olympic record until 1960 at Rome. German and Negro American congratulated each other and strode to the dais arm in arm to receive their medals. The crowd roared their approval and in retrospect the incident only serves to make one wonder at how events in Germany proceeded as they did.

Jesse Owens had won two gold medals in as many days and the following day he made it three. He reached the final of the 200 metres on a cold, showery day and after some delay while the leaders of the 50 kilometres walk entered the stadium led by the Briton Harold Whitlock, the runners got to their marks. The wind was spiteful and cutting across the track but Owens seemed to run through it all, unbothered. He went two yards clear at the halfway mark and through the tape in 20.7 seconds. It was the first time that any man had run the 200 metres curved race in under 21.0 seconds. Robinson of the United States gained the silver and the Dutchman, Osendarp, took the bronze. The German crowd rose to greet the 'Tan Streak from Ohio State'. They cared nothing for his colour, only that they had been privileged to witness one of the world's greatest athletes in action.

Jesse Owens's gold medal exploits did not end there, either. Along with Metcalfe he was called up to run in the 4 x 100 metres relay. In the heat he helped the Americans to equal the world record of 40.0 seconds; in the final he saw to it that they clipped two-tenths of a second off that record. Jesse Owens joined Alwin Kraenzlein as the only Americans to win four Olympic golds in one Olympiad. The inclusion of Owens and Metcalfe in the relay caused some controversy as they were in the team at the expense of the Jewish runners, Sam Stoller and Marty Glickman, though if the Jews were excluded to please Hitler, he can hardly have been overcome with joy at two Negro replacements. Owens, like so many American athletes, found himself with problems after the Olympics. He was suspended by the AAU for refusing to tour Sweden and on his return home he turned professional, raced against horses and worked for a time with the Haarlem Globetrotters. He was one of the greatest athletes of all time, but he was still a blackman in a less than tolerant country. He spoke volumes when he said later, 'Sure I wasn't invited to shake hands with Hitler — but then I wasn't invited to the White House to shake hands with the President of the United States either.'

# BUMP THAT COST WOODERSON DEAR

Sydney Wooderson of Blackheath Harriers was one of the outstanding milers in the world between the wars. For five years, from 1935 to 1939 inclusive, he won the AAA's mile championship; and in 1937, at Motspur Park, Surrey, he lowered the world record to 4min 6.4sec. But despite his fine pedigree as a miler, Wooderson, small and bespectacled, failed to win the two honours which would have meant so much to him — a gold medal in the Olympic Games 1,500 metres, and victory in the Princeton 'Mile of the Century'. A pulled muscle robbed Wooderson of his chance in the 1936 Olympics in Berlin — when New Zealander Jack Lovelock took the gold in the 1,500 metres — and the Helsinki Olympiad, scheduled for 1940, fell victim to the ravages of World War II. In the 'Mile of the Century' it was a tragic accident which left unanswered the question of whether this small, insignificant looking Englishman who would be immediately lost in a crowd, was good enough to take that other crown.

Sydney Wooderson had already declined two invitations to compete in the Princeton event, like Lovelock before him finding his business commitments too pressing to allow him to undertake the long journey across the Atlantic. But the Americans were ever keen to include the world's best in their Princeton mile so that the race might live up to its grand title. They had been desperate to tempt Wooderson after his world record and in 1939 the Blackheath man finally felt able to accept. The news was greeted with immense excitement in the United States, for with the world record holder competing against the best Americans, there was every possibility that the Palmer Stadium track, one of the fastest in the world, might see yet another

barrier lowered. Already, Lovelock had smashed the record there in 1933 and Glenn Cunningham, whose record Wooderson had eclipsed, had done the same to the New Zealander's time in 1934 on the same track.

Wooderson, like Lovelock before him, arranged a series of races to prepare himself for the big Princeton test. The first of these saw him run a mile in only one second outside his record at the Whitsuntide meeting at the White City. His training was under the watchful eye of the fine miler, Albert Hill, the Polytechnic Harrier who had won the AAA's mile in 1919 and 1921. Everything went according to schedule and on the eve of his departure for the United States, Wooderson decided to make an attempt on the three-quarter mile world record at Manchester. Beside the world mile record, Wooderson also held the 800 metres world record — 1min 48.4sec at Motspur Park in August 1938 — and the 880 yards world record broken the same day, and held the belief that the three-quarter mile event would sharpen him up for the Princeton meeting with the best of the Americans. Wooderson did more than sharpen himself up at Manchester that day. He smashed the world record and became the first man to run that distance in under three minutes.

The following day Wooderson, his brother Stanley, and coach Albert Hill set sail for America. Wooderson had allowed himself only a few days acclimatisation before the big race, reasoning that a short interval would suit him better than having to wait two weeks or more when the strange conditions might affect his peak fitness. In his training runs on the Princeton track Wooderson both impressed and surprised the American sportswriters who found it difficult to believe that so slight a figure could possess such power in his legs. The goal of every miler was now the sub-four minute mile and Americans everywhere speculated on the possibility of the magical barrier at last being broken. Certainly, they had every reason to believe that another world record was in the making.

Wooderson's rivals included Glenn Cun-

*Sydney Wooderson, seen here winning a thrilling race against Willie Slyhuis of Holland to set a new British record of 13min 53.2sec for the three-miles in the AAA Championships at the White City in 1946.*

ningham, hero of many desperate struggles on the track and winner of the Princeton mile in 1935 and 1938, as well as being a former world record holder; Archie San Romani, a 26-year-old New York University student who had triumphed in the 1937 'Mile of the Century' and then come runner-up to Cunningham a year later; Chuck Fenske was described as the successor to Cunningham and he had impressed English spectators the previous summer when he visited the United Kingdom; and the field was completed by Blaine Rideout, one of the famous twins from North Texas. Just before half past five on the sultry afternoon of 17 June 1939, the runners came out on to the Princeton track and were greeted by a noisy welcome from some 28,000 spectators. The temperature was in the high nineties, hardly conducive to running

fast times, and as the runners went to their marks they heard the rumble of distant thunder.

San Romani was in lane one, Cunningham in the second, Wooderson in the third, Fenske in the fourth and Rideout in the fifth and on the outside. The starting gun echoed — and was immediately followed by another, nearer, clap of thunder — and the runners were off and into the first lap. Wooderson, his long, raking stride swallowing up six feet of track with each bound, went straight into the lead, followed by Cunningham, Fenske, Rideout and San Romani. Halfway round the first lap Rideout passed Fenske but with the first circuit completed there was little between Wooderson in the lead and the back-marker San Romani. It was a disappointing quarter for those hopeful of a new world record,

39

taking 64 seconds which suggested no new time. Though it was not Wooderson's original intention to set the pace, the Americans refused to pass him and throughout the second lap the little Englishman found himselt out there at the head of the field. The halfway stage was reach in 2min 8sec — another 64-second quarter — and it was anybody's race, though as they went into the third quarter Cunningham — who on his own admission some days earlier, was not in top form — began to fall back.

The third lap was up in 65 seconds — 3min 13 sec for the three-quarter mile — and Cunningham had now dropped back to fourth place behind Wooderson, Fenske and Rideout with San Romani still bringing up the rear. It stayed like this for another two hundred yards, but it was now clear that the Americans would have to make the challenge immediately if they were not to allow Wooderson to pull away from them. English radio listeners were straining their ears, praying that the radio waves would not peter out at this vital moment, when they heard commentator Ted Husing cry out 'Wooderson's out! He's been tripped! He's been tripped!'

It was a tragedy for the little English runner who had threatened to capture the hearts of all America. Blaine Rideout was the villain of the piece as far as Englishmen were concerned. In attempting to pass Wooderson on the outside it appeared that the North Texan had cut across the world record holder with the result that they bumped. The result was that Wooderson was thrown out of his stride and before he could regain his balance the other runners had swept past him. In a race he had led from the start, Wooderson now had to swallow the bitter pill of finishing last. As he reached the tape he was in a state of near collapse, not so much from physical weariness but from utter mental desolation at what had happened.

Immediately Rideout went across to him and offered an apologetic hand at what had happened. It was a tragedy, of that there was no doubt, but it was also an accident, the kind of thing that could happen in almost any race. This Wooderson accepted. Meanwhile, Fenske had won the race in 4min 11sec, well outside the world record, to be followed by Cunningham, San Romani and Rideout. Wooderson went on to do well in longer events after the war — but the tantalising question of whether this brilliant English miler would have taken the 'Mile of the Century' will never be answered. There are those who feel he would; and there are those who consider Wooderson to have been on the verge of defeat anyway as Rideout made his challenge. A chance collision was enough to leave it to the history books which can only record one of sport's most fascinating imponderables.

# THE FLYING DUTCHWOMAN

At the 1936 Olympic Games in Berlin, an eighteen-year-old Dutch girl called Fanny Koen was entered for the high jump. No one expected her to win and indeed she finished sixth equal with a best jump of two inches below the 5ft 3in shared by three winners. Those girls went into a jump-off — won by the Hungarian Ibolya Csak with 5ft 4in — and Fanny Koen, having already exceded the expectation of her coach, Jan Blankers, then took part in the 4 x 100 metres relay as part of the fifth-placed Dutch team. Twelve years later, Fanny Blankers-Koen — she married her coach in 1940 — was back at the Olympic Games, now a thirty-year-old housewife who had been largely written off by the sporting press, despite coming to London as the world record holder in 100 metres, 80 metres hurdles, and both the long jump and high jump, together with shared relay records. She set aside the criticism and went on to become the toast of London, the Flying Dutchwoman who lit up the austere capital still emerging from six years of a long, dreary and bloody war.

Francina Koen was a schoolgirl when her father noticed that she had an aptitude for sports. Proud father pushed his daughter hard and before long she was acknowledged as one of Holland's great future hopes in the 800 metres. She was noticed by the former Dutch triple jump champion, Jan Blankers, and he took her under his wing. Soon Blankers realised that Fanny would not make the international grade at 800 metres and he felt that she was more suited to the high jump. Hours of coaching and training paid off and in 1936 the young Jewish girl went to Nazi Berlin where she did much better than anyone expected. One year later

Fanny was a member of the newly-formed Sagitta Club of Holland, and here Blankers decided that she must develop her sprinting. In June 1938 his decision was more than justified when Fanny Koen ran 11.0 seconds for the 100 yards to equal the three-year-old world record set by South Africa's Barbara Burke in Pretoria.

Fanny Koen's world seemed bright and full of hope. Yet there were the darkest clouds imaginable on the horizon. In 1939 Germany invaded Poland and the world was plunged into its second great war in a generation. In the first few months of 1940 it became increasingly clear that the Low Counties were coming under threat and so it turned out. Fanny Blankers-Koen and her fellow Dutch were under the heel of the Nazi jackboot. All this, together with the birth of her son, Jan, in 1941 left little time to devote to athletics. In 1942, however, with life now settling down again to some kind of normality, or at least consistency, under the German occupation, she began to train once more. In September of that year, Fanny ran 11.3 seconds for the 80 metres hurdles in Amsterdam to equal the world record held by Italy's Testoni who had twice run that time. In 1943, Fanny broke both the high jump and long jump world records. In Amsterdam on 30 May she cleared 1.71 metres (5ft 7.37in) for the high jump; and in September, at Leiden, she took the long jump record to 6.25 metres (20ft 6in). In May 1944, back in Amsterdam, she took the world 100 yards record with 10.8 seconds. The war ended, but the birth of her daughter, Fanny, came too close to the 1946 European Championships in Oslo to allow Fanny senior to break any world records, though it did not prevent her from winning two gold medals in the 80 metres hurdles and the 4 x 100 metres relay.

In 1948 London staged the first Olympic Games for twelve years. The 1940 Olympiad had been scheduled first for Tokyo and then for Helsinki before it became obvious that there would be no Games, and the 1944 Games were never even considered. Towards the end of 1945, London applied for the 1948

Games, despite strong opposition from some quarters, and in March the following year learned that it had been awarded them. The London organisers, however, planned no grand event on the scale of Los Angeles and Berlin. Existing facilities, based primarily on the Empire Stadium at Wembley, would be used. In 1908 the Games were also staged in London at a centre originally built for an exhibition. Again the London Games would live up to Olympic expectation.

On Thursday, 29 July 1948, King George VI declared the Olympic Games open. Fifty-nine nations had sent between them 4,030 men and 438 women competitors, though there were notable absentees. It was far too early for either Germany or Japan to be considered; and the Russians, who had not competed in the Olympic Games since 1912, were not affiliated to the IOC and could not, therefore, take part in any of the events. These Olympic Games needed a cracking start and on the very first day of the track and field events they were blessed with a magnificent final when the Czech, Emil Zatopek, smashed the Finnish hold on the 10,000 metres, setting such a pace that the world record holder, Heino, was forced to drop out. Grey, drab post-war London warmed to these Games at once. They were exactly what the nation needed after all those years of deprivation. On the last day of July, a Saturday, they produced yet another great star who proceeded to warm the cockles of thousands of British hearts. Within the space of seven days, the name of Fanny Blankers-Koen would be on the lips of every Briton with access to a wireless set, newspaper, and, of course, a ticket to the Olympic Games.

Fanny had sorted out her events for London well in advance and had decided to concentrate on the 100 and 200 metres, the 80 metres hurdles, and the 4 x 100 metres relay, leaving aside the long jump. In her individual events, Fanny was seeded to run in the first heat each time. The first was the 100 metres and she went out of the blocks like a rocket, streaking through in 12.0 seconds with the other runners left trailing in the wake of her long blonde hair. The time was well outside her own world record but Fanny Blankers-Koen had shown that, despite her age, she was going to be a difficult opponent to beat. Dorothy Manley managed to get within one-tenth of a second of her time, but no sprinter in the heats could better it and Fanny took the Sunday off to reflect on what lay ahead.

The next competition day was August Bank Holiday Monday and, naturally, it rained. Fanny clocked 12.0 seconds again in the 100 metres semi-finals, a fine performance in view of the wet track, and four-

*Fanny Blankers-Koen takes the second hurdle during the first round heat of the 80 metres hurdles at Wembley when she set a new Olympic record of 11.3 seconds. In June 1948 the Flying Dutchwoman had set a new world record of 11 seconds in Amsterdam.*

tenths of a second behind her was Australia's new hope, Shirley Strickland. Fanny still had the best time of any of the semi-finalists and she was expected to walk away with the gold medal. She did just that, equalling the Olympic record of 11.0 seconds and finishing three yards ahead of the silver medallist, Dorothy Manley, and the bronze medallist, Shirley Strickland, both of whom were credited with 12.2 seconds. The following day saw the first heats of the 80 metres hurdles and now the rain had ceased there was the possibility of a fast time. Fanny obliged, ghosting over the hurdles in the first heat to set a new Olympic record of 11.3 seconds. The semi-finals were held later that afternoon and Fanny took her race with 11.4 seconds. Maureen Gardner, the girl who was most fancied to test Fanny, finished third in her semi-final after knocking over two hurdles. Shirley Strickland won in 11.7 seconds but Fanny knew that both these girls would test her in the final itself.

Next afternoon the runners lined up. Fanny Blankers-Koen in lane one, the British girl, Maureen Gardner in lane two. King George VI and Queen Elizabeth were due at the stadium to add to the tension of the occasion and when the gun cracked, Fanny's customary rocket-like start failed her. It was Maureen Gardner who got away to the roars of the home crowd, and Shirley Strickland was in second place. But the Dutch housewife gathered up all her experience and slipped into the right gear. At the fifth hurdle she was level with Gardner when what could have been disaster struck. Fanny hit the flight and was thrown off balance for a split-second. She recovered, drove hard for the tape and hurled herself through it neck-and-neck with Maureen Gardner. Fanny felt sure that she had done enough to take the gold medal, but only the eye of the photo-finish camera would decide for certain. There was a cruel moment when the British national anthem was played — had Gardner done it after all? — but it was to herald the arrival of the king and queen.

After an agonising wait the girls numbers were placed on the scoreboard. After the first two digits of the winning number, Fanny, number 692, knew that she had taken her second gold. She and Maureen Gardner, the silver medallist, both had the same time of 11.2 seconds and thus shared the new Olympic record; Shirley Strickland was two-tenths of a second behind them. Fanny Blankers-Koen was both elated and deflated. She now had two gold medals, but her thoughts now turned to the morrow and the heats of the 200 metres. She now found herself under the most incredible pressure. With victory in every one of her races so far, she was beginning to succumb to the inevitable rigours of the occasion. Yet she went through her heat of the 200 metres in 25.7 seconds, hardly challenged by the other girls. But then the pressure began to build up again. In the next six heats, Fanny's time was beaten no less than four times with the South African, Daphne Robb, best in 25.3 seconds. Fanny could only stand and watch and eventually she could bear to do that no longer. She went to the comparative calm of the dressing room and burst into tears. It was the best thing that could have happened to the housewife from Holland. She sobbed and sobbed, weeping uncontrollably until all the tension had flooded out through the tears. At last there were no more tears — and no more tension. Refreshed and revitalised Fanny Blankers-Koen went out to the Wembley track and won her semi-final in 24.3 seconds, a good six yards ahead of her nearest rival and, most important of all, a second faster than her heat time.

The second semi-final was a much closer run thing and Shirley Strickland ran a great race. But so too did Britain's Audrey Williamson and even the camera could not decide the winner. The result was a dead-heat, but the time was over half a second slower than Fanny's. It was a great psychological boost for the Flying Dutchwoman and she looked forward to the 200 metres final the following day with her confidence brimful.

Daphne Robb, who finished third in that semi-final with a time of 25.1 seconds, drew the inside lane for the final, with Fanny on the outside lane. The day was wet, the track hardly suitable for a fast race. None of this mattered to Fanny, however. From the gun she streaked away to win in 24.4 seconds, seven-tenths of a second behind was silver medallist, Audrey Williamson who was separated from bronze medallist, American Audrey Petterson, only by the camera, with Shirley Strickland in fourth place. Fanny Blankers-Koen, the woman who was written off as too old to compete, had taken more gold medals than any other woman. She still had the 4 x 100 metres relay to which to look forward. This time she was not involved in the first heat where Canada earned a surprise win over Australia, though only by one second. Austria and Great Britain went through from the second heat and then the Dutch girls — Xenia Stad-de-Jong, Jeanette Witziers-Timmers, Gerda Van der Kade-Koudjis and Fanny Blankers-Koen — won their heat in a time that was three-tenths of a second faster than the Canadians.

The Dutch were in fourth place when Fanny received the baton on the last leg of the final. She passed the second and third-placed girls and drew level with Australia's Joyce King ten metres from the tape, accelerating still faster and going over the line to win another gold medal. The time was 47.5 seconds, more than a second outside the Olympic record, but that did not matter. The Flying Dutchwoman had entered four Olympic events and won four gold medals.

Fanny Blankers-Koen went home to a rapturous welcome, but far from retiring she went on to break the 220 yards world record in 1950, won the 100 metres, 200 metres, and 80 metres hurdles at the European Championships in Brussels, and at the age of thirty-three took yet another world record in the pentathlon in Amsterdam in September 1951. The 1952 Helsinki Olympics saw her compete sixteen years after her Olympic debut, though a blood infection saw her lose all her titles she had sought so ambitiously to defend. It was a sad end to a great career, but most people choose to ignore Helsinki and remember instead London in 1948 when Fanny Blankers-Koen lit up the grey skies and overcame her tears to become a golden champion four times over.

# CABRERA AND MATHIAS SEAL A MEMORABLE GAMES

The athletics events at the 1948 Olympic Games in London's Wembley Stadium were watched by what was then the largest aggregate Olympic crowd on record, with thousands more locked outside the gates of the Empire Stadium inside, where the likes of Emil Zatopek and Fanny Blankers-Koen were thrilling the crowds. But the last two days of those Olympic athletics, which previously had been overshadowed by the deeds of the Czech champion and the Flying Dutchwoman, served up their own memorable moments to provide a fitting finale for a magnificent Olympiad. The heroes were a small Argentinian and a seventeen-year-old youth who had suffered from anaemia as a child. These two perhaps unlikely champions took gold medals in two of the sport's toughest and most demanding events. They provided an already epic Olympiad with more classic moments.

The story of that teenager who overcame a childhood illness to win his chosen sport's ultimate prize was a real sporting fairytale. It started in a small Californian town and went on until the youngster reached the pinnacle of success, starred in the Hollywood version of his own life story, and became a United States Congressman. Bob Mathias was born in Tulare in November 1930. As a child he suffered potentially crippling anaemia, but so determined was he to recover fully that by the time he reached his sixteenth birthday, Mathias held the Californian schoolboy discus record. In June 1948 — two months before the London Olympics and five months before his eighteenth birthday — Mathias took part in his first decathlon and won the first of ten such competitions that he contested from then

until 1956. Less than eight weeks after his debut in what is surely the most demanding and searching test of track and field skills, Mathias was on his way to Britain with the rest of the American Olympic team. Fresh out of school he was but yet a boy; and yet he was about to become the youngest Olympic male champion in the history of athletics — and he was going to do it in a 'man's' event. It was going to be one of the most outstanding feats in the history of the modern Olympic Games.

For Mathias, the Olympic Games started towards the end of the athletics programme. In the first section of the competition, held on Thursday 5 August 1948, there were five events. In the first of these, the 100 metres, Argentina's Kistenmacher won in 10.9 seconds to give himself 872 points; Clausen

*Bob Mathias winds himself up to hurl the discus.*

of Iceland clocked 11.1 seconds (814 points); Simmons of the United States, 11.2 seconds (787 points); Mullins of Australia 11.2 seconds (787 points); Mathias also 11.2 seconds (787 points); and Heinrich of France with 11.3 seconds (760 points). The long jump found its leader in Adamczyk with a best jump of 7.08 metres (23ft 2.75in) which gave him 825 points. Heinrich jumped 6.895 metres (22ft 7.25in), giving him 775 points; and Mathias could not get into the first six places. In the shot Mathias collected 719 points with an effort of 13.04 metres (42ft 9.25in), though he was placed fifth in that event which was won by Gierutto of Poland with 14.53 metres (47ft 8in). The high jump found Mathias one of five athletes who tied on 1.86 metres (6ft 1.25in); and in the last event of the day, the 400 metres, the young American collected 780 points with a time of 51.7 seconds. Kistenmacher picked up most points — 845 — with a time of 50.5 seconds and it was the Argentinian who led the day with a grand total of 3,897 points. Heinrich was second with 3,880 points and young Bob Mathias third on 3,848. Two other Americans, Simmons (3,843) and Mondschein (3,811) lay fourth and fifth.

The Olympic record of 7,900 points, set by the United States' Morris in Berlin in 1936, did not look to be in danger as the decathletes resumed their battle on the following day. What a dreadful day it was! Rain, mist and an occasional gust of wind turned the competition into a nightmare. But Olympic rules declared that the decathlon must be competed inside two days — so on they pressed. The first event of the day was the 110 metres hurdles and Mullins of Australia took that with 15.2 seconds and 896 points. Mathias collected 818 points with 15.7 seconds, while Heinrich went one-tenth of a second better and earned 833 points. Throughout the day the thirty decathletes hurled the javelin, threw the discus, and pole-vaulted through the heavy rain; and they splashed around a half-flooded track. They looked a sorry sight, sodden shorts clinging to their aching legs. By 9.15pm they were still vaulting, only it was now difficult to see the bar from the

stands. The orange flash of the starter's gun showed up in the gloom as another 1,500 metres got away; and there were the vaulters again, this time lit by a temporary arc lamp.

Mathias's performance on this second day were as follows: In the 1,500 metres he did not finish in the top six; in the pole vault he claimed 692 points with a leap of 3.50 metres (11ft 5.75in) and in the javelin he was again unplaced in the first six. But in the discus, his best event, Mathias was the outstanding performer. His 44 metres (144ft 4in) gave him 834 points and put him well ahead of the next best discus thrower — Gierutto who took 765 points with a throw of 41.80 metres (137ft 1.5in). It was the discus which shot Mathias into an overall lead which he never lost. Some twelve hours after the first decathletes had got down to their marks for the 110 metres hurdles, the last competitor completed his tenth event and Bob Mathias was declared the overall winner with 7,139 points. Heinrich took the silver with 6,974, and Simmons the bronze with 6,950. The crowd which witnessed the final act of this saga was naturally much smaller in number than that which had settled down earlier in the day. Yet those brave few who huddled under the Wembley stands as midnight approached were rewarded with one of the most outstanding moments of any Olympic Games. Bob Mathias became the youngest man ever to win an Olympic athletic title. From then on he was the top decathlete in the world. He went on to break the world record three times and successfully defended his Olympic crown in Helsinki in 1952. He forfeited his amateur status the following year — though he continued to compete in the American armed forces — and became a film star in his own life story and entered American politics. The boy from Tulare who suffered from anaemia had grown up in a red-blooded American of the most stirring kind.

The excitement was not yet over for the London crowds of 1948. On the day following Mathias's splendid triumph, the marathon was run. Yet again there was to be a special hero in this most famous of all races, and yet

*Mathias launches himself into the long jump.*

behind. Gailly's nearest rival at this stage was the Chinese Lou. The front men twisted and turned along the course before reaching the Elstree war memorial where the order was Gailly, Lou, Guinez (Argentina) and Josset (France) followed by the Swede, Oestling, and the Argentinian, Delfo Cabrera. In the stadium itself a great cheer went up when it was announced that Holden had moved up into seventh position. Choi, one of three Koreans in the marathon, and Luyt of South Africa, had both joined the leaders on the return journey from Radlett and along the main road which ran through Elstree. There now began a mile-long climb, followed by a run downhill, but it was at this point that the patient crowd back at Wembley learned that their great favourite, Jack Holden of Tipton Harriers, had retired. It was later learned that Holden was suffering from a combination of a stomach upset and blistered feet.

There were now some four and a half miles to run and Choi now took the lead to revive memories of 1936 when another Korean, Kitei Son who was representing Japan, brought the Olympic record under two and a half hours when he won the gold medal from the sturdy little Briton, Ernie Harper of Hallamshire Harriers. Now, with the thirty-eight-year-old male nurse Tommy Richards, who had started his running career in cross-country in Wales, moving up to fifth place, it began to occur to everyone that history might be repeating itself. But Gailly now made a heroic effort to regain the lead and in doing so he pushed the Korean back down the field. Back once more in the stadium, the questions were being asked: Where were the Finns — above, all the great Heino? Surely he would be in contention. Sadly, that great runner had badly miscalculated his tactics and was already a spent force. He would not enter the Olympic arena until the marathon had been drained of all its excitement and drama.

Now it was announced that the leading runner was in the Olympic way and making his way towards the arena. But the announcer tantilisingly did not reveal his identity —

again there was to be a story of tragedy. All of it culminated in a cracking finish inside the stadium when a race which had taken over 26 miles to run was won in the last few yards. Forty years earlier, twenty-seven runners from twelve countries had started the Olympic marathon from Windsor Castle. Led by Dorando they had finished it in epic style at the White City Stadium. Now, almost half a century later, forty-one runners represented twenty-two nations as the marathon crocodile went out of Wembley Stadium, into the suburbia of north-west Middlesex, and then into the semi-rural sprawl of Hertfordshire before winding its way back towards the great stadium where thousands waited for news of just who was leading this most heroic of races.

At the halfway stage the leader was the former Belgian paratrooper, Etienne Gailly, who was over half-a-minute clear of his nearest rival and over two minutes ahead of the leading British hope, Jack Holden. The Belgian retained his lead and with about seven miles left to run it was still Gailly with Holden still apparently running strongly in eleventh place and now only a minute who could it be? When the spectators did catch their first glimpse of the leader they saw the figures 252 on his red vest and knew that it was the gallant Belgian, Etienne Gailly. He entered the stadium a few yards ahead of the Argentinian, Delfro Cabrera. The sight of the tottering Belgian must have been very like the entrance of Dorando forty years earlier. He could make little progress at all and in a flash the Argentinian was past him and heading for the tape; then came Richards, just twenty seconds behind and, like Cabrera, looking full of running. There was now just one lap to negotiate — though it must have seemed like an insurmountable obstacle. Cabrera pulled away and headed for home; Richards came after him some fifty yards in arrears. The Argentinian steamed supremely past the line and the Welshman came in just sixteen seconds later to take the silver medal. It was a bonus for the British crowd, but now their eyes turned to see if poor Gailly, the man who had burned himself out when killing off the Korean challenge, could win the bronze. Other runners were now entering the stadium — Coleman, the South African, who finished sixth in Berlin; his fellow Springbok, Luyt; and the Argentinian Guinez. But Gailly, though he tottered and at one stage seemed to have given up, bravely made it home in third place much to the relief of the crowd. Delfo Cabrera's time was 2 hours 34min 51.6 sec which was nearly six minutes slower than Son's 1936 record. Those last 400 metres of the Wembley track had been an agonising path for the Belgian; for Cabrera, who finished so strongly, they must have appeared as light as air. It was a fitting climax to a great Olympiad.

# ZATOPEK'S IMPOSSIBLE TREBLE

Helsinki, Sunday, 20 July 1952. Seventy thousand people, packed into the Olympic Stadium, rise to their feet to acclaim the son of an impoverished Moravian carpenter. The man wears the red vest of Czechoslovakia, his arms flail out in a style which makes athletics coaches avert their gaze, his face wears an agonising expression, teeth bared, tongue lolling out of the side of his mouth. But his expression belies his state. Emil Zatopek, one of the greatest distance runners of all time is in no pain. He is just about to do what everyone expects of him — to win the 10,000 metres on the opening day of the Fifteenth Olympiad. Before these Helsinki Games are over, Zatopek will win two more races to accomplish what everyone thought up until then was an impossible treble. The former army corporal who rose to the rank of major is about to enter the world of sporting legends.

Finland, of course, had been the dominant power in distance running for almost four decades of Olympic competition and it was fitting that the opening ceremony of the Helsinki Games should feature two of the greatest Finnish runners of all time. Paavo Nurmi was the man chosen to carry the Olympic torch through the gates of the stadium and ignite the Olympic flame; and it was Hannes Kolehmainen who trotted up the steps to light the second flame atop the traditional tower. Since the 1912 Games, Finland had produced the very best in the distance events and as the rain swept down over the Helsinki Stadium on that July day in 1952, generations of Finns — and others — who were not born when Kolehmainen took the gold in both 5,000 and 10,000 metres in Stockholm, nor perhaps even when Nurmi

was doing great deeds in 1924 and 1928, felt privileged to witness the last Olympic appearance of this great pair. Within the period of these Games they would also be privileged to bear witness to another great Olympic champion who was to assume the mantle of the greatest distance runner the world had seen for a generation.

Emil Zatopek was eighteen years old when he finished second in a cross-country race at Koprivnice. He was working in a shoe factory while he saved up enough money to enrol for a trade scholarship and before long the ambitious young Czech had earned himself a college degree. At the same time Zatopek was becoming more and more interested in the science of athletics — one of his specialist subjects was chemistry and he put his academic training to the best possible use as he devised new athletics training methods, setting himself the most punishing schedules and noting the way in which his body reacted to them. In concert with this, Zatopek was now gaining some spectacular successes on the track and in 1944 he broke the Czech records for 2,000, 3,000 and 5,000 metres. In 1945 Zatopek found himself in the Czech army and again broke the 5,000 metres record. He was a natural selection for the 1946 European Championships in Oslo, finished fifth in the 5,000 metres and once more beat what was now becoming virtually his own property, the Czech national record for that distance. Two years later, and after more arduous training, Zatopek arrived in London for the 1948 Olympic Games where he won the 10,000 metres with the greatest possible ease, ghosting past rival after rival to take the gold medal in 29min 59.6sec. He took the lead in the tenth lap and ran everyone else, including the world record holder Viljo Heino, into the ground.

Zatopek was now emerging as one of the great distance runners. Between London and Helsinki he broke the world record for the 10,000 metres no less than three times, until in August 1950, at Turku in Finland, he lowered it to 29min 2.6sec. In addition he also had the world records for the 20,000 metres which he broke twice in the same month with a best of 59min 51.8sec at Stara Boleslav in his native Czechoslovakia; for the 10 miles — 46min 12sec in the same race on 29 September 1951; and for the longest distance run in one hour — 12 miles 809 yards, again during that race. A year earlier, during the European Championships in Brussels, Zatopek had taken the 5,000 metres title twenty-three seconds ahead of the silver medallist; and in the 10,000 metres he lapped every other runner in storming to another European title. He had also found time to marry Dana Ingrova, Czech javelin thrower, who was to join him at the 1952 Olympics.

So, the only question which the spectators asked themselves as Zatopek lined up for the 10,000 metres on the opening day in Helsinki was simply to ponder if the Czech, now thirty years old, his hairline receding, would break the world record once more. There seemed no doubt that he would win; nor any doubt that the Olympic record would be broken. Five of his opponents that day had been inside thirty minutes for the distance, but Zatopek's record still seemed unassailable by all but the man himself. For the first two laps Zatopek was content to let Les Perry of Australia make the running. In the third lap the thirty-two runners became stretched out and Perry fell back while the Russian, Aleksander Anufriyev, took up the lead. Zatopek tucked himself into ninth position, moved up to eighth during the fourth lap, threaded his way still nearer the front during the next lap, and during the sixth circuit burst to the front. He now set a telling pace. Gordon Pirie, Britain's one real hope of a medal, tried to stay with him but could not stand the blistering run and he too fell away. Zatopek was now remorselessly destroying all challengers, though with his head rolling from side to side and wearing that pained expression he looked to be in trouble himself. But this was the hallmark of the Zatopek style. After ten laps and 4,000 metres, the Czech clocked 11min 45.6sec. By the seventeenth lap the Frenchman, Alain Mimoun, the 1948 silver medallist, was still making a game fight of it. Mimoun had tried

hard from very early on, but now he too was outdone. After twenty-one laps, the French challenge was also over and Zatopek scorched round in an average 71 seconds before an amazing last lap of 64 seconds saw him through the tape in 29min 17sec. It was a new Olympic record, though outside his world record, and it was almost another sixteen seconds before the second man, Mimoun, crossed the line. Emil Zatopek had done what everyone had expected of him. Now he immediately turned his attentions to the 5,000 metres. In 1948 the Belgian, Gaston Reiff, had beaten him for the Olympic gold by no more than a yard with a most devastating final 200 metres.

Zatopek's first task was to qualify for the final. He was scheduled to run in the third heat and watched while Mimoun won the first and just failed to beat the Olympic record; and as the German, Herbert Schade, did pass the Olympic record mark. Zatopek's heat was eagerly awaited and he treated the race with an almost unreal indifference. The Olympic champion Gaston Reiff had contented himself with merely qualifying from his heat; now Zatopek chose to do the same. He allowed the Russian, Anufriyev, to lead the early way, then speeded up to take four runners, including Britain's Chris Chataway with him and away from the rest, and then sent the Russian away to win the heat, coasting into third place himself and making certain that the Swede, Albertsson, was given second place though both men recorded the same time.

By the time Emil Zatopek was ready for the 5,000 metres final, his wife, Dana, had herself won a gold medal in the javelin. These were happy days for the Zatopek family and Emil could not have wished for a bigger boost as he lined up for the gun. The early leader was Chris Chataway, speeding away from the starting line in fast time with Zatopek again quite happy to nestle in the front bunch. In the second lap, Schade took over from the Briton. This is how it went until the seventh lap when Zatopek decided to make some of the running himself. He did the circuit in sixty-eight seconds before

*Chris Chataway hits the kerb and falls as Emil Zatopek takes round Mimoun of France and Schade of Germany on his way to the 5,000 metres gold medal at Helsinki.*

allowing Schade to assume the vanguard. At the 3,000-metres mark it was Schade, Reiff, Chataway, Zatopek and Mimoun, with the leader clocking 8min 30.4sec. Britain's Gordon Pirie came up from the back to take the lead for a short while, but then Schade reassumed control. At the bell the pattern changed rapidly. Pirie dropped right away and out of the race, Reiff, too, lost touch with the leaders. Three hundred metres from home and with the runners still playing cat and mouse, Chataway decided to go for bust. He surged forward, taking Zatopek and Mimoun with him, and now the final act was about to be played out. Zatopek and Mimoun went past Schade but for Chataway disaster struck. The exhausted Briton had given his all and stumbled blindly against the track-side kerb before crashing to the ground. Zatopek stormed down the straight, hitting the tape five yards ahead of little Mimoun for a new Olympic record of 14min 6.6sec. Pacemaker Schade took the bronze medal and Pirie came up to fourth with a limping Chataway just behind him.

Emil Zatopek had two gold medals and the question now on everyone's lips was whether he would try for the marathon. 'Why not?' asked Zatopek, and what was more, he felt that a time of two and a quarter hours was quite possible, and that after admitting that he had never run a competitive marathon! To underline the audacity of that remark we can also consider that Jim Peters had, that very year, run a world best time for the marathon — 2hr 20min 42.2sec — well outside anything like the two and a quarter hours which Emil Zatopek apparently considered was there for the taking.

He was fortunate with the weather on the day that the 1952 Olympic marathon was due to be run — it was cool and cloudy, the sort of conditions for which marathon runners pray. Jim Peters was there as Britain's leading hope; so too was the 1948 Olympic champion, Delfo Cabrera of the Argentine. Peters led the field at what seemed like a ridiculous pace, but at the 10-kilometre mark it was still Peters in the lead, sixteen seconds ahead of the Swede, Gustaf Jansson, with Zatopek waiting in third place. After 20 kilometres, both Swede and Czech had left the Englishman some ten seconds in their wake and Peters later told the story of how Zatopek had asked him, 'Can't you go any faster?' before speeding past the agony-wracked Londoner. At the 30 kilometre stage — about eighteen miles — Zatopek went in front with Jansson second, Peters third and the 1948 champion, Cabrera, coming up hard on the Englishman's heels. Cramp eventually forced Peters to retire, but Zatopek knew nothing of that. He forged ahead and entered the stadium to tremendous applause. He had opened up a gap of two and a half minutes and passed the line in the new Olympic record of 2hr 23min 3.2sec, more than six minutes inside the old record. Argentina's Gorno came in some 800 yards behind Zatopek to win the silver medal, and Jansson was third just in front of the Korean, Yoon Chil Coi. Emil Zatopek went on to many more world records, but he will always be synonymous with Helsinki and the accomplishment of the 'impossible treble'.

# BANNISTER CLIMBS THE EVEREST OF ATHLETICS

Of all the many great duels fought out on the athletics track there can be no event which evokes greater excitement and passion than the mile. People who have absolutely no interest in the sport will still be able to tell you if the world record for this Blue Riband of the track is broken. On a wet and blustery May afternoon at Iffley Road, Oxford, in 1954, 25-year-old Roger Gilbert Bannister ran himself into the realms of immortality by becoming the man to win, not just another mile race, but the race for what had become almost the Holy Grail of athletics — the first mile to be run inside the seemingly impossible four-minute barrier. Bannister, fourth in the 1952 Olympics 1,500 metres, probably realised that this would be his last chance; and he and two colleagues, Chris Chataway and Chris Brasher, both fine international athletes themselves, set about their task of taking Bannister through that magical four-minute barrier. They saw to it that the race to become the first man to eclipse both the nine-year-old world record and four minutes was won by a Briton, though the Australian John Landy, and the American Wes Santee, had both threatened to do the same. Bannister's feat will be remembered for all time, for it was the climax of a battle which had started almost seventy years earlier.

The story really begins in 1886, though it was probably not realised at the time, when Walter George, 27-year-old Wiltshire-born athlete, ran a mile in the then astonishing time of 4min 12.8sec. George had already achieved an incredible record as an amateur runner with world records in the mile, 2 miles, 3 miles, 6 miles, 10 miles, and the longest distance run in 1 hour, as well as practically every English title from 880 yards to 10 miles, as well as cross-country. His mile record of 4min 18.4sec was set in 1884 — the same year as all his other world records were set — and two years later George, by now a professional, pitted himself against the Scottish holder of the world professional record, William Cummings, who had run the mile in 4min 16.2sec. In 1885 George had beaten Cummings in 4min 20.2sec; in 1886 he destroyed the Scotsman and claimed a new world record which would not be bettered for almost forty years — that was a measure of how far George was ahead of his time. In 1885 he had been timed at 4min 10.2sec for six yards over a mile during a time trial!

It was not until 1915, when the American N.S. Taber ran with the aid of pacers, that George's record was virtually equalled; and 1923 before the great Finnish runner, Paavo Nurmi, established a world record with 4min 10.4sec. That left 4min 10sec as the new target at which every international miler aimed, but not until 1931 was that barrier broken when the Frenchman Jules Ladoumegue ran 4min 9.2sec and, in fact, Ladoumegue was also the first man to beat Nurmi's eight-year-old record. By now, the 1,500 metres had been introduced to competitive athletics. The distance is some 120 yards shorter than a mile, but naturally it attracted men who were already world-class milers. Nurmi and New Zealand's Jack Lovelock each set world records for the shorter distance and there were people — and still are, for that matter — who tried to convert the time taken to run 1,500 metres into the time it would have taken to run the mile. Thus the athletics world had metric races which were described as the 'equivalent' of a such-and-such mile. In 1937, the great British miler Sydney Wooderson clipped the world record down to 4min 6.4sec and between 1934 and 1940, the 4min 10sec barrier was broken many times by people like Wooderson, Lovelock, the Americans, Bonthron, Cunningham, San Romani, and Lash, and the Italian Beccali.

Wooderson's 1937 record was the race which now made athletics turn its mind to

*Roger Bannister crashes through the tape at Iffley Road after breaking the four-minute barrier.*

the possibility of a sub-four minute mile, though it has to be said that the thoughts were only whispered at first. But during World War II, the deeds of two Swedish runners, Gunder Hagg and Arne Andersson, turned possibility into probability. In 1942 both men beat Wooderson's mile record — Hagg had eclipsed the Briton's 1,500 metres record in 1941 — and the race was on. Hagg broke the world record again — in 4min 4.6sec — and then he returned from a trip to America to find that Andersson had lowered that to 4min 2.6sec. The battle between the two Swedes was a phenomenal duel, marred only by the fact that the rest of the world was locked in war, and in 1944, it was Andersson again in 4min 1.6sec, though Hagg himself passed the old world record in 4min 2sec. Then, in July 1945 in Malmo, Hagg won an epic race in 4min 1.4sec to end the battle and set a world record which lasted until Bannister broke it in 1954. The suspension of Andersson and Hagg, and the retirement of

Wooderson, effectively checked the race for a mile in even time.

Other runners did try before Bannister — Sweden's Eriksson did 4min 3.1sec and Gaston Reiff of Belgium 4min 2.8sec — but it was not until Bannister, Landy and Santee that the sub-four minute mile became, once more, a reality. Since the age of twenty, when he clocked 4min 11.1sec for the mile, Roger Bannister had been considered a potential world-beater. In the 1950 European 1,500 metres he finished a close third and then improved his mile time to 4min 9.9sec. One year later that time was down still further — to 4min 7.8sec — and then Bannister went to Helsinki for the 1952 Olympic Games. Shortly before the Games, Bannister ran a three-quarter mile time trial in 2min 59.2sec which was almost four seconds faster than the unofficial world record held by Andersson. We all felt that Bannister could now get among the Olympic medals but the large number of entries for the 1,500 metres meant that an extra round was included at relatively short notice and Bannister could not cope with three hard, nerve-wracking races in three days. He finished fourth — behind Barthel (Luxembourg), McMillen (United States) and Lueg (Germany) — in the UK record time of 3min 46sec. A measure of how far standards had improved was the fact that the first eight men home all beat Lovelock's 1936 Olympic record time of 3min 47.8sec.

So to that cold, windy day in Oxford on 6 May 1954. Bannister knew that the sub-four minute mile was now possible — though Hagg's 1945 record had stood for so long that the four-minute barrier was beginning to assume an almost mystical dimension. It was so near — and yet Bannister now had a best time of 4min 2sec; but John Landy had run that time on about half a dozen occasions, and Wes Santee had clocked 4min 2.4sec. Bannister's best time, which made him the joint third fastest miler in the world, came at Motspur Park, Surrey, on 6 June 1953. Alas, the authorities refused to accept it as a British record because of the lack of serious competition and the fact that the race had been conducted with an element of secrecy. One month previously, in a match against the University at Oxford, Bannister had run a superb race in 4min 3.6sec, despite facing a stiff breeze for some of the way. So, Bannister, Landy and Santee were all within sight of the apparently insurmountable. Now it was Bannister's turn to see what he could do.

The occasion was the annual match between the Amateur Athletic Association and Oxford University — the match in which Bannister had run 4min 3.6sec just twelve months earlier. The meeting did not start until five o'clock that afternoon and when it did the weather could hardly have been less conducive to the running of a world record. Bannister and Chris Chataway knew the track well from their Oxford days; so did Chris Brasher who had run here as a Cambridge student at St John's College. For the first hour of the meeting there was an uneasy atmosphere over the rain-lashed Iffley Road stadium, for everyone sensed that there was something very special about the mile due to be run at around six o'clock. For Oxford there was little early success. C.E.E. Higham's splendid time of 14.8 seconds in the high hurdles, only inches behind the AAA champion, P.H. Hildreth, was one Oxford highlight, and I.H. Boyd won the half-mile to make up for his lack of success, through injury, in the University Sports.

But all this was largely academic and pushed to the back of the mind when the six runners made their way to the line for the start of the mile. A glance at the programme showed that R.G. Bannister, C.J. Chataway, W.T. Hulatt and C.W. Brasher represented the AAA; G.F. Dole and A.D. Gordon wore the University vest. As if it sensed the importance of the occasion, the weather settled down and with the rain ceased and the wind quieted, the gun sent the six men on their way. The plan was that Brasher, 'always a gallant and willing runner or steeplechaser' according to the following day's edition of *The Times*, would set the pace and this the bespectacled runner did. He completed the first quarter of a mile in 54.7 seconds, taking Bannister along in 57.7 seconds. There were

but a couple of strides between Brasher and Bannister, and between Bannister and Chataway, and that was how it remained throughout the second lap. At the half-way point the clock read 1min 58sec, within the rate required, and now Brasher fell away, his task completed, and it was Chataway who moved into the lead, still dragging Bannister with him. Chataway made his charge halfway down the back straight during the third lap and at the bell Chataway clocked 3min 0.4sec with Roger Bannister just one-tenth of a second behind him.

It was again in the back straight where the race changed complexion once more. This time it was Bannister who passed the hare and went into the lead. Chataway, too, was spent and Bannister now forged ahead on his lonely race against the clock. Further and further ahead went Bannister with an ever-lengthening stride which gobbled up the damp track yard by yard. The spectators, some 1,200 of them, now knew that they were witnessing a run of potentially epic proportion. Bannister went through the tape some fifty yards ahead of Chataway before collapsing into the arms of race officials and supporters. This had been an incredibly fast race; but had Roger Bannister done enough to break that magical four-minute barrier? The word swept round that he had, but there was still no official confirmation. Then Norris McWhirter teased the crowd with his anouncement: 'Ladies and gentlemen, here is the result of event number nine, the one mile.' The crowd now hushed and McWhirter went on: 'First number forty-one, R.G. Bannister of the Amateur Athletic Association and formerly of Exeter and Merton Colleges, with a time which is a new meeting and track record and which, subject to ratification, will be a new English native, British national, British all-comers, European, British Empire and world record. That time is THREE . . . .' The rest of McWhirter's words were lost in the general cheering, in fact the time was 3min 59.4sec. Bannister had done it! After nine years of trying the world record had been broken and with it the barrier which had defied the greatest milers in the world.

*Roger Bannister wins the mile race at the 1954 AAA Championships at White City in a time of 4min 7.6sec.*

Bannister had clipped almost two seconds off the old record but amid all the acclaim he was the first to acknowledge the great debt he owed Chris Chataway (who finished second in a personal best time of 4min 7.2sec) and Chris Brasher. From Aabo, Sweden, John Landy, who himself planned three attempts on four minutes that June and July, cabled: 'Bannister's world record is terrific. I send him my warmest congratulations.' From Santee came a similar message: 'It was a great performance. Of all milers Bannister is the one I would just as soon have seen break four minutes.' From Boston, the Olympic 1,500 metres champion J. Barthel of Luxembourg, who was studying at Harvard, said: 'We can relax a little now. Bannister merits this more than anyone else. I would have loved to have been the first man to do it but Bannister loves to run and he is a lesson to every athlete.'

Roger Bannister had opened the gates and within seven weeks of his epic performance, John Landy had run even faster. Since then, sub-four minute miles have become almost commonplace, and yet they still command attention. There is still something special about it, like no other event, time or distance. Bannister's career was not over with his Iffley Road run, however, and in the Commonwealth Games in Vancouver that year he beat Landy in his fastest time of 3min 58.8sec and in one of the most thrilling mile races ever seen. Then Bannister took the European 1,500 metres title in this his last season. Dr Roger Bannister was knighted in 1975 but even that honour can not have meant more to him than on that cold May evening at Oxford twenty-one years earlier when he put behind him the disappointments of Olympic failure and instead wrote himself an indelible entry in the history of athletics.

# GREATEST MILE OF THEM ALL?

Just forty-six days after Roger Bannister's epic run at Oxford in May 1954, the Australian John Landy ran a mile in 3min 57.9sec, to clip 1.5 seconds off Bannister's record. That was on 21 June and less than eight weeks later the pair were due to meet head-on in the Empire (as they were called then) and Commonwealth Games in Vancouver. The feats of Bannister and Landy, the only men to have run a mile in under four minutes, meant that the final of the Commonwealth Games mile was, perhaps inevitably, billed as the 'Mile of the Century'. Of course, there had been many such 'Miles of the Century', especially when the Americans ran one every year in the 1930s at Princeton. But now the often abused title took on a new and significant meaning. Here were the two fastest men in the world over a mile; both had run the distance in shattering times — and now there was the ultimate duel.

The gold medals had been well-divided on the Thursday of the Games — 5 August 1954 — with England taking the shot and long jump, Australia the javelin and the women's 220 yards, New Zealand the men's 220 yards, South Africa the women's javelin, Jamaica the 120 yards hurdles, and Northern Rhodesia the women's 80 metres hurdles. The Duke of Edinburgh and Earl Alexander of Tunis were among the 20,000 crowd who saw several records broken, including Mrs M. Nelson of Australia, running in what she claimed was her last individual race before retirement, who set a new world record of 24 seconds for the 220 yards, although with a following wind she had to wait a while to see if that record would be ratified. The wind had gusted in excess of two metres a second on occasions and several 'records' had

already been disallowed. This, too, was the day of the mile heats. The favourites to qualify were, of course, Bannister and Landy, but both had to run faster than was expected in order to do so. Bannister's heat was won by Halberg of New Zealand in a new Games record of 4min 7.4sec. The Australian, Warren, had set an early pace for the first half mile before dropping out; and Ferguson of Canada was hard on Halberg's heels, to be followed by Bannister who jogged the last few yards while keeping an eye on the runners behind him. England's D.C. Law finished fourth to qualify.

Bannister had been suffering from a cold for much of that week but he declared himself fit and had shown that he had much in reserve for the real battle two days hence. John Landy, meanwhile, had an even easier task in qualifying from his heat. The race was run in much slower time than Bannister's heat and W.D. Ballie (New Zealand), V. Milligan (Northern Ireland) and Landy were all together at the tape and each was credited with the time of 4min 11.4sec. Landy, too, gave the impression that he had much in reserve for Saturday's race, but the Canadian, Ferguson, and the New Zealander, Halberg, had also signalled that they would be challenging hard, though it was still difficult to imagine that the final would be anything more than a two-horse race. At the end of the day England, with sixteen gold medals, led the field with 378½ points, followed by Australia (254¾ points and fifteen golds), Canada (234 points and eleven golds), South Africa (168¾ points and six golds), and New Zealand (112¾ points and five golds). There were also golds for Northern Ireland, Scotland and Trinidad (two each), and Jamaica, Nigeria, Southern Rhodesia and Northern Rhodesia (one each). The Northern Rhodesians would also have claimed a world record when Miss E. Maskell took the 80 metres hurdles in 10.9 seconds, but that gusting Canadian wind ruled out the ultimate achievement.

All this, important though it was to the individuals concerned, paled by comparison with the race that everyone had been waiting two months to see — the final of the mile where the two fastest men in the world were to meet head-on. The runners came out on to the track before 32,000 spectators who craned their necks to seek a better view of the race which might, if any did, deserve the title of 'Mile of the Century'. From the gun New

*Roger Bannister wins the Commonwealth Games mile from John Landy in Vancouver.*

Zealand's W.D. Baillie raced away into a startling lead, but he was soon overhauled by John Landy who then set a cracking pace, taking the rest through the first 440 yards with his own time a very fast 58.2 seconds. Landy continued his punishing schedule throughout the second lap and increased his lead to some ten to twelve yards. The half-mile stage was reached by the Australian in 1min 58.3sec and still he enjoyed that comfortable lead. Perhaps, just perhaps, thought the spectators, Bannister, suffering as he had been with that cold, could not find the reserves to make this a race.

But into the third lap Roger Bannister began to close the gap between himself and the flying Australian. Landy was still fighting it out with his shorter, quicker steps, but Bannister was edging ever nearer with that long smooth stride with which he was now so firmly identified. The gaps between the two men closed throughout that third lap, foot by foot, yard by yard, until, at the bell — a still startling time of 2min 58.4sec — they were virtually neck-and-neck, though Bannister still gave away the slightest edge to Landy. Into the final straight they raced, now absolutely shoulder to shoulder, and at the last bend Bannister now took the lead with Landy apparently lost and looking over his left shoulder as Bannister came up to pass his right hand. With 100 yards left to run Bannister now forged ahead. Landy, meanwhile, had obviously given his all and he had nothing left with which to force a final spurt from his body. Roger Bannister breasted the tape five yards ahead of Landy — but the Australian himself still broke through the four-minute barrier.

Bannister and Landy had accomplished the second-fastest mile in history. Bannister's time was 3min 58.8 sec, obviously a personal best and a new Games record — well over eight seconds faster than the previous record set by Halberg in the heats. Landy had produced a magnificent 3min 59.6sec in taking the silver medal and it was announced that his time at 1,500 metres had been 3min 41.9sec, only one-tenth of a second outside his own world record which had been set at

Turku, Finland, during the race which also gave him the world record for the mile. Bannister seemed a little distressed as he crossed the line but happily he soon recovered and was the first man to shake Landy's hand. The two men who had made this 'Mile of the Century' live up to its name then jogged around the Vancouver Stadium for some fifteen minutes to prevent their muscles stiffening. It was also a lap of honour and they were acclaimed in the most enthusiastic manner, the cheers which greeted them surpassed even those for the Canadians' own darling, Ferguson, who had surprised even himself perhaps by taking the bronze medal in a time of 4min 4.6sec.

The world had waited for such a race and they had been amply rewarded. The post-race comments of the two athletes make interesting reading and Bannister revealed that he had decided to run the race his way and not to be influenced by the other runners, even Landy. He told *The Times* correspondent at the Games: 'I ran my own race all the way. I was not going to allow any other runner upset my plans. I hoped to run a 3min 59sec mile and I did not alter my training plans one bit. Landy set my pace and I knew that I was going to win halfway through the final lap. That I ran a 3min 58.8sec mile pointed out to me once again the value of a regular training programme. I was not as tired today as I was the first time I broke the four-minute mile. I ran faster over the last one hundred yards at Oxford, but the race itself was slower. I finished relatively fresh this time and I could have knocked another second off if I had started my kick sooner.'

Landy said that he knew his hopes of beating Bannister faded when he failed to lose the Briton in the first three-quarters of the race: 'I tried to set a fast pace from the start and I did exactly as I wanted, but I was beaten by a better man on the day.' John Landy also spoke of that incident on the final bend when he looked for Bannister: 'I knew someone was coming up on me hard — and I knew that it must have been Roger Bannister. I was not worried about anyone else — just Bannister. I could hear him coming up behind me, but I was unsure as to how far he was away. I decided to look over my shoulder to check — and when I did he wasn't there!' Bannister was in fact passing Landy on the outside and as the Australian commented: 'When I looked back in front of me, Roger Bannister was a good stride in front and going away strongly. He deserved to win.'

So the 'Mile of the Century' had perhaps proved to be just that. After the furore had died down, and in the comparative calm of the dressing room, Roger Bannister was asked if he thought that he could lower the mile barrier still further: 'Records are made to be broken,' he told the questioner, 'The human spirit is indomitable. There will never be a time when the human spirit will not be able to better these marks.'

# CHATAWAY'S FIRE TAMES KUTS

In May 1954, a red-haired 23-year-old athlete from the Achilles Club helped Roger Bannister to become the first man to run a mile in under four minutes on a windy early evening at Iffley Road, Oxford; the following month that same flame-haired runner helped Australian John Landy to lower Bannister's world record on a June evening in the Finnish city of Turku. In October of that year, on a fine autumn night under the floodlights of London's White City Stadium, he pushed aside one of the world's greatest long distance runners to assume his own mantle of glory. Chris Chataway, for so often the man who helped others to world records, took one of his own.

Christopher Chataway was born in Chelsea on the last day of January 1931. An Oxford student with Bannister, he knew the Iffley Road track well when he pushed his former student colleague through the four-minute barrier, but it was at longer distances that Chris Chataway had made his name. In the 1952 Olympics in Helsinki, he had competed as a raw and inexperienced 21-year-old and paid the penalty for his lack of know-how at international level by tripping over the bend of the track during the 5,000 metres final which was won by the great Emil Zatopek. Chataway finished fifth — though there are many runners who would not have had the courage to pick themselves up in the same way in which Chataway did — and went away to ponder on the lessons which he still had to learn about the cut and thrust of world-class running. In 1954, now a much more experienced runner, Chataway, took the gold medal in the Commonwealth Games three miles at Vancouver in a time of 13min 35.2sec; and a few weeks later he came as

near to a world title as ever he would with a silver in the European Championships 5,000 metres in a race won by Kuts in 13min 56.6 sec — a new world record for that distance.

Kuts was *the* long-distance runner of the times and his taking of that world record in Berne on 29 August 1954 came as no surprise; it also took away from Chris Chataway the three-miles world record which the Briton had held jointly with another Briton, Frank Green, when they together clocked 13min 32.2 in London in July of that year. Kuts's new record was 13min 27.4 sec. The 5,000 metres record which Vladimir Kuts broke was previously held by Emil Zatopek, and before him Gunder Hagg, so Chataway was in the highest company. Now the Achilles man had an opportunity to prove himself against the Russian when all athletics looked forward to the projected match between London and Moscow, to be staged at the White City Stadium on 13 October 1954. It was a meeting which captured the imagination and some 40,000 spectators were present to see a splendid match which, although the Russians won quite easily, produced two memorable races and gave Christopher Chataway a world record in the most thrilling manner imaginable.

For the record Moscow won all but one of the field events, both of the hurdles and relay races, and the 100 metres, 400 metres and 1,500 metres to win by 103 points to 56. In the women's match Miss J.C. Desforges, later to become Mrs J.C. Pickering, emulated her form in the European Championships and took the long jump ahead of the Russian champion, A. Chudina, though London still lost that match by 56 points to 32. But British fans could put the overall defeats behind them and concentrate on the two great individual victories by the London team. The first of these came in the 10,000 metres where Ken Norris of Thames Valley Harriers, who twenty-four hours earlier had been a doubtful starter due to a badly blistered foot, triumphed with a brilliant performance. For a good two-thirds of the race Norris was content to shadow the Russian champion of 1953, Anufryev; the other leading Russian,

Sandor, was also happy to tuck inside and leave the pace-making to the champion.

During the fifth mile Norris took over the lead and from that point until about 1,000 yards from home, he and the Russian exchanged the lead until Norris at last decided that it was time for him to make the break. Norris established for himself a ten-yard lead and before the runners had entered the last lap, Sandor had also passed Anufryev. Norris now romped away, finishing forty yards ahead of Sandor with Anufryev a further forty yards behind him. Norris's time of 29min 35.4sec was the fastest ever run in Britain at the time and the fact that both Russians also beat the previous record merely underlined just what a terrific performance Norris had achieved. All this was done with a badly blistered heel! After Norris decided to take up the lead for good the Russians had no way of preventing him from taking the race and the crowd who sat somehow aloof in the shadows, brought themselves back into the action by roaring the Londoner home.

This then was a tremendous fillip for Christopher Chataway when he came out for the start of his 5,000 metres duel with Vladimir Kuts. Norris's had been an exceptional performance, but it was the 5,000 metres which the crowd had awaited with great expectancy. Kuts, the 27-year-old from Aleksino, had replaced Emil Zatopek as the great long distance runner of the age. He had a reputation of setting an early blistering pace and then 'blowing up', but when he took the record in Berne in August that year, he opened up a considerable gap between himself and Chataway and Zatopek, a gap which he never surrendered. Chataway knew that to win this race he would have to stay with Kuts, no matter what kind of pace the Russian set for him to follow. He knew that he must always keep in touch; for if Kuts was allowed the luxury of a lead, the like of which he had engineered for himself in the European Championships, then Chataway would never catch him. The weather had held fine for the meeting and the conditions were as pleasant as an October evening in London can be as Chataway, Kuts and the rest of the field jogged nervously around the start, awaiting the call to draw swords.

As expected Kuts went away to a blistering start and the first mile was covered by the Russian in 4min 24.4sec, though the important factor, so far as the Londoners were concerned, was that Chris Chataway passed that first mile stage only a pace or two adrift of the front-runner. Indeed, Chataway had dragged the rest of the field along with him so that the fourth-placed man at the stage, who was the other Russian, V. Okorokova, was only five yards behind his colleague. At this point Kuts decided to make the supreme effort and go away from the rest of the field to set up a winning lead. Chataway refused to be left behind and he went with the Russian, though by now he was leaving the rest of the field behind. Once more during that second mile, Kuts stepped up the pace; but once more Chris Chataway upped a gear himself and as the two front ment passed the two-mile stage with Kuts leading Chataway by a few feet, the time was a fast 8min 54.6sec. The pace was crippling and the crowd watched anxiously for the first sign that one or the other of these two magnificent athletes was beginning to feel the strain. That sign never came and at the bell Kuts actually speeded up again. Yet again Chataway went with him and the two men were now more than 100 yards ahead of the third man, Driver of London who battled along gamely, but long since out of the main race and fighting only a personal battle with Okorokova for third place.

So often Kuts had killed off his opponents with searing bursts of speed but on this October evening the flame-haired Chataway had no intention of letting the Russian leave him for dead. The crowd roared Chataway on as the men entered the final lap and still the pace was absolutely killing. But with twenty yards to go, Chataway, far from flagging, found something from somewhere and forged ahead towards the tape. In the end it was Chataway who showed the world that he had greater reserves of strength and he crossed the line just a couple of feet ahead of Kuts. It had been an epic race, described at the time as possibly the greatest ever seen on a British track, and the times tell their own story.

Chataway's time of 13min 51.6sec beat the world record set by Kuts in Berne; Kuts, too, had beaten his own world record with a time of 13min 51.8sec; and it was revealed that when the Russian crossed the three-mile stage, still in the lead, he had broken the world record for that distance with a new time of 13min 27sec. It was a brilliant victory by Chataway and he had achieved it with a brand of raw courage at the most vital moments, keeping within range of Kuts every time the Russian tried to break clear; indeed, Kuts must have found it so demoralising that every time he felt that he had done enough, he found only that Chataway was still there. They called Chataway the 'Red Fox' and Kuts the 'Iron Man'. On this occasion it was the wily and courageous Englishman who found enough metal to beat the world. Kuts in fact took the world record back almost immediately and Chataway held the title for only ten days. In Prague, on 23 October, Kuts ran the 5,000 metres in 13min 51.2sec. The two men each held the three-mile world record in turn after that, Kuts lowering his own record still further to 13min 26.4sec during that Prague 5,000 metres ten days after the White City classic, and Chataway taking it down to 13min 23.2sec in London the following July. Chris Chataway will always be remembered for two things: His part in the first sub-four minute mile — fittingly he passed that barrier himself in 1955 — and that courageous

*Chris Chataway breaks the tape ahead of Vladimir Kuts to win an epic 5,000 metres at the White City.*

epic at the White City when he topped the world, albeit briefly, with one of the greatest performances that British athletics fans have ever seen.

# KUTS THE IRON MAN DOES THE DOUBLE

The great Melbourne Cricket Ground, scene of many exciting matches between Australia and the other Test-playing countries, is an unlikely place to play host to a Russian long distance runner's greatest triumphs. But in November 1956, when the Olympic Games were held in the Southern Hemisphere for the first time — and consequently were also staged very late in the year — the vast Melbourne stadium was the scene of just such a triumph when a 29-year-old athlete from Aleksino emulated another great Iron Curtain runner, Emil Zatopek, and took the Olympic Games 5,000 metres and 10,000 metres titles with two of the most astonishing displays of running from the front that athletics has ever seen.

Vladimir Kuts began running in 1949 at the age of twenty-two. Four years later, Kuts arrived on the international scene and was earmarked as the natural successor to Zatopek, the man who had accomplished the 'impossible' treble of 5,000 metres, 10,000 metres and marathon in the 1952 Helsinki Olympics. In 1953, Kuts won his first national titles and he was unofficially timed at 13min 31.4sec for three miles during a 5,000 metres race — a whole second faster than Gunder Hagg's world record. The time was not ratified and it was Great Britain's Chataway and Green who jointly broke that record the following year. But Kuts's time was almost due and in the 1954 European Championships in Berne, he not only took the 5,000 metres gold medal, but broke the world record for both that event and the three miles. Kuts broke away from the rest of the field and won the race by a wide margin from Chataway and Zatopek. Six weeks later Kuts lost the 5,000 metres record in a classic race at the White City (chronicled elsewhere in this book) but in doing so he again lowered the three-mile record; and ten days later the Russian reclaimed his 5,000 metres record. Kuts lost the 5,000 metres record once more when Britain's Gordon Pirie beat him in Norway in June 1956; but just prior to the Melbourne Games, Kuts broke the world record for 10,000 metres with a time of 28min 30.4sec.

This, then, was the pedigree of the man who was favourite to take at least one of the two golds in the 5,000 and 10,000 metres in Melbourne. Kuts's early reputation had been that of a runner who tried to put so much of a gap between himself and the rest of the field that his efforts often ran opponents into the

*Vladimir Kuts, the Iron Man.*

ground, though occasionally he would, himself, 'blow up' and lose the race. Kuts had little time to waste before attempting the first leg of the Olympic double when, on the very first day of the athletics events — 23 November 1956 — he lined up for the final of the 10,000 metres. British hopes lay largely with Gordon Pirie and Ken Norris. Pirie, of South London Harriers, had reached international level in 1951 and was the man who brought British track distance running out of the doldrums. Not since the great Sydney Wooderson had Britain enjoyed such a revival of its flagging distance fortunes. In 1951, Pirie took his first AAA title — the six miles — in an English record time, and

although he took more national records in 1952, he was not ready for the Olympics and finished fourth in the 5,000 metres and seventh in the 10,000 metres.

Pirie's 1953 season was a fantastic success for the Leeds-born runner. He took the first of three successive English cross-country titles, broke the world six-miles record with 28min 19.4sec — clipping more than eleven seconds off Heino's 1949 record, helped Britain to a new world record in the 4 x 1,500 metres relay, and beat Wes Santee, America's great miler, in 4min 6.8sec. Pirie then inflamed the critics by suggesting that he would one day run the 5,000 metres in 13min 40sec — the world record then stood

*Gordon Pirie, the South London Harrier, was beaten twice by Kuts in Melbourne, but the Briton was a fine runner. Here, thousands of miles from the Melbourne Olympic Stadium, he splashes round the White City to win a two miles race.*

at 13min 58.2sec — but three years later, in Bergen on 19 June 1956, the South London Harrier did just that; he defeated Kuts and took the world record in 13min 36.8sec. Pirie had not finished! Within three days he equalled Iharos's 3,000 metres world record when he ran 7min 55.6sec at Trondheim. Pirie then ran 3min 43.7sec in winning the 1,500 metres; and in Malmo, on 4 September, he lowered the world record for the 3,000 metres to 7min 52.8sec, running against a field which included Sandor Iharos, Laszlo Tabori and Istvan Rozsavolgyi, the great Hungarian trio.

This was the battle for which British athletics had waited — Pirie, the man who held the world record for 5,000 metres, against Kuts, the world record-holder over 10,000 metres. There could hardly have been a more potentially memorable start to an Olympiad. Yet surely Kuts was the man for this particular race? Pirie was a world-beater up to 5,000 metres, but Kuts was the much stronger man over the longer distance. The commentators now felt that perhaps Pirie should have remembered this in the summer when he ran so many under-distance races. Kuts knew it too and from the start he set out to burn up his rivals. The Russian went straight into the lead from the gun and defied any man to get in front of him. None could. At 5,000 metres, Kuts had disposed of all his rivals save Gordon Pirie. But Pirie was having the punishment meted out to him too and the blonde Russian, head rolling from side to side, began a series of brutal thrusts to dispose of his last challenger. Down the back straight — Kuts's favourite killing ground — Pirie found the pace intolerable. Then this incredible Russian invited Pirie to take over and in the twentieth lap the Briton actually went into the lead for a short spell. But Kuts knew his rival and simply waited for him to fade. The end was not long in coming. The hammering which Pirie had taken now told and as the two men passed the post for the twenty-first time, Pirie suddenly slowed. All the strength seemed to drain from the Yorkshireman's body and he had all but given up. Away went Kuts,

storming ahead now like a true Olympic champion. The Russian had not beaten seventy seconds since the seventeenth lap but now, with Pirie vanquished, he clocked 69, 69, 70 and finally 67.6sec.

Kuts took the gold medal with a new Olympic record of 28min 45.6sec, though he was outside his own world record. In fact, the first six men home all passed Zatopek's Olympic record of 29min 17sec, and there was a surprising battle for the silver and bronze. As Kuts broke the tape, Jozsef Kovacs of Hungary, the first man to beat Zatopek over 10,000 metres, and Australia's Allan Lawrence, entered the home straight. It was Kovacs who got the silver by just two yards, the Australian taking the bronze. Ken Norris finished in fifth place in 29min 5sec, but for poor Pirie there was no glory and he fell away badly to finish in eighth position. For all of twenty-one laps Pirie had stayed in contention; every time Kuts had kicked, Pirie had gone with him. But the crippling pace had finally told and Pirie could now only dwell on the 5,000 metres to come. For Kuts there was the inevitable lap of honour, which the surprisingly fresh-looking Russian took with obvious relish, and then there was the withdrawal into the inner self and the preparation for the second part of this historic double attempt.

The 5,000 metres heats were run in three races with the first five in each heat qualifying for the final. Pirie won the first heat in 14min 25.6sec and in the second heat, Kuts took the field round until the last two laps when the home favourite Lawrence, perhaps overcome by the encouragement of the crowd, suddenly surged forward. The Russian was happy to let him go and Lawrence won the heat in 14min 14.6sec with Kuts second in 14min 15.4sec. The two other Britons, Chris Chataway and Derek Ibbotson, also qualified quite easily and on 28 November 1956, they and the other runners warmed up on the track which had been specially built around this famous old cricket ground. Britain, with three top class runners including the world record-holder, felt that they must have a real chance of a gold medal.

For Kuts there was the thought that when he won the first track gold medal of the Games in the opening 10,000 metres, he had also become the first Russian to win an Olympic track gold, and, of course, it was Vladimir Kuts who the crowd wanted to see. The whole day's events had been built up around the 5,000 metres final and the Russian was the star, even before the gun cracked to send the runners away.

At the gun, another Russian, Chernyavskiy, led round the first turn but by the end of that bend there was the inevitable sight of Kuts, head rolling slightly, coming up to take over the lead even at this early stage. He took the field around the first 400 metres in 63.4 seconds and behind him at the post were Pirie, Tabori and Ibbotson. The second and third laps were run in 66 seconds apiece, and the fourth in just one second slower. Kuts, Pirie, Ibbotson were the front three with Chataway still in contention tucked nicely in at eighth spot. The Russian now put in one of his spurts, followed by another, and after seven laps it was still the scarlet vest of the Soviet Union in front, but now trailed by three white British vests as the others began to feel the pace. Kuts's tactic was to lose everyone and so far only the Britons had succeeded in not being shaken off. After eight laps still more runners were dropping among the stragglers — the Australian Thomas, and the old Hungarian fox, Szabo, among them. Chataway had taken over from Pirie in second place, but the red-haired former Oxford man was about to be overcome by stomach cramps and would fall away rapidly before the ninth lap was finished.

Kuts now stepped up the tempo once more and the ninth lap took only 65 seconds as the Russian suddenly grabbed a further five yards with a spurt around the bend. Pirie retrieved them but thoughts now went back to the 10,000 metres when similar tactics had destroyed Pirie. The tenth lap took 69 seconds and it was here that the final order was sorted out. Kuts simply stormed away, leaving Pirie and Ibbotson to fight out the silver and bronze between themselves. Poor Chris Chataway was now some fifty yards adrift and falling still further away. The penultimate lap saw Kuts go round in 66 seconds and at the bell this incredible Russian had opened up a gap of some forty yards. His last lap took just 62.6 seconds — it was staggering that a 5,000 metres should be won by a front runner who then put in an even more devastating spurt as he neared the tape. He broke the tape at least eighty yards ahead of the battling Britons. His time of 13min 39.6sec beat the Olympic record by no less than twenty-seven seconds. Meanwhile, Ibbotson took over the lead in the race for the silver, but with twenty yards to run, Pirie put in his own searing burst of speed and went through in front while Ibbotson, his face screwed up in anguish, dropped almost to walking pace as he took the bronze in his despair. British athletics has been so used to disappointments and here was yet another. The cream of British 5,000 metres running had been soured by this amazing iron man from Russia. Vladimir Kuts died of a heart attack in August 1975, aged forty-eight. His name will live for ever as the man brave enough — and great enough — to lead from the front.

# CHRIS BRASHER'S LONGEST HOURS

At just after six o'clock on the evening of Thursday, 29 November 1956, a pleasant, bespectacled man was ushered into a room at the Melbourne stadium which was playing host to the 1956 Olympic Games. It had been a cold, windy, dull day out there on the running track. Now the atmosphere was charged with high tension as Christopher Brasher, the Briton first past the post in the final of the 3,000 metres steeplechase, was about to enter another battle just as tense as the one from which he had emerged victorious out there on the windswept Melbourne arena. Brasher had still not received his gold medal. Shortly after crossing the line he had been staggered by a loudspeaker announcement which told him that he had been disqualified. He went quickly over to ask just what had happened and was told that a referee, after hearing a version of events from a barrier official, had disqualified the Briton for impeding the Norwegian, Ernst Larsen, and that the gold medal would now be hung around the neck of the Hungarian favourite. It was a cruel moment and although the British team manager, Jack Crump, had immediately lodged an appeal, it seemed that all Brasher's efforts in becoming a story-book Olympic champion had been in vain.

The plain fact was that Brasher never expected to even be at the 1956 Olympic Games, never mind take a gold medal. John Disley, 1952 bronze medallist in Helsinki, and Eric Shirley, who finished the 1955 season with a new British all-comers' record of 8min 47.6sec, had been chosen by the selectors and it was only after the British Olympic budget yielded more money than was originally anticipated, that Chris Brasher was added to the team. Brasher had been Disley's number two at Helsinki — chosen for those Games before he had represented his country in an international — and had qualified with a run inside the Olympic record which Iso-Hollo had set in Berlin in 1936. In the final Brasher had crashed against a solid hurdle, but fought gamely on to finish eleventh out of a field of twelve. Now his steel was to be tested again.

Brasher's name will always be bracketed with the first sub-four minute mile run by Roger Bannister at Iffley Road, Oxford, in May 1954, when he and Chris Chataway acted as pacemakers for the first successful attempt on that magical barrier in time. But the oil company executive who ran with his spectacles taped firmly to his head, had always been, at heart, a steeplechaser. He was born in Georgetown, British Guiana, in 1928 and at school at Rugby had won himself the reputation of being a tough, rugged sportsman who liked nothing better than a challenge against all the odds. Nothing says more for the Brasher character than the fact that he took up mountaineering and once found himself on the short-list for an assault on that other apparently unconquerable peak, the tip of Mount Everest.

After Helsinki, and then the Bannister mile, Chris Brasher concentrated on qualifying for the Olympic Games to be held in Australia in 1956. In 1952 he had been the second string to John Disley; now Eric Shirley, with that new British all-comers' record in the year before the Melbourne Games, had arrived on the scene to threaten Brasher's ranking. Even a run which lowered Shirley's record was not enough to oust that athlete. In August 1956, just three months before the Olympic Games, Brasher had got inside Shirley's time by four-tenths of a second. He had not, however, won the race. That went to Disley with a new record of 8min 46.6sec — a whole second faster than Shirley. The world record, meanwhile, was falling even faster. First the Russian, Semyon Rzhishchin, ran 8min 39.8 sec; then the Hungarian, Sandor Rozsnyoi, lowered that to 8min 35.6sec. Chris Brasher was well down the rankings and it was only that last-minute financial hiccup which earned him a reprieve and a place in the British party which headed down to Australia at the start of the English winter.

The Austrian coach, Franz Stamfl, had helped Bannister and company to prepare for that historic mile at Oxford; now it was Brasher who went to him for personal help and advice in the run-up to Melbourne. Brasher's first few days in Australia saw him win a two-mile race at Geelong where he clipped a full six seconds off the Australian record. It was exactly the right kind of fillip which the runner needed and two weeks later, on 27 November 1956, he found himself with a second piece of good fortune when the draw for the 3,000 metres steeplechase heats put him in the 'easier' of the two, facing Shirley, Rzhishchin, Heinz Laufer of Germany, and the Australian, Neil Robbins, while in the first heat, Disley faced Ernst Larsen and, Hungary's Rozsnyoi, the world record holder, Larsen set a cracking pace in that heat and led early on until both Disley and the Hungarian went past him and through the tape in the same time — 8min 46.6sec. Shirley took a slower heat in 8min 52.6sec, with Rzhishchin second and Laufer, Brasher and Robbins also qualifying in that order.

Two days later, Brasher lined up in the middle of a row of runners to contest the 3,000 metres steeplechase final, though well down the list of favourites for a medal. After all, there was the British hero, John Disley; there was the world record holder, Sandor Rozsnyoi; there was the Russian, Semyon Rzhishchin, who had himself held the world record for thirty-three days before the Hungarian took it from him; there was the Norwegian, Ernst Larsen; even Eric Shirley. No, there seemed no point in thinking that the 28-year-old Brasher might bring honour to his country, though it is said that his room-mate in the Olympic village, Chris Chataway, had ordered a bottle of the best champagne — just in case! Perhaps Chataway knew of the immense efforts that Franz Stamfl had put into preparing Brasher for this race; perhaps he had seen at first hand the effect which the great Austrian athletics tutor had made on Brasher. Whatever the reason for Chataway's optimism, it was not going to be misplaced.

The gun cracked and many people in the stadium did not hear it as the sound was carried quickly away on the gusting wind. They did see, however, Disley and Larsen get away to a fast start and for the first 200 metres the Norwegian led the way, setting the same fierce pace he had done in the first heat. Disley followed him and behind the British favourite came a string of runners Rzhishchin, Rozsnyoi, then Brasher, followed in turn by the American, Jones, and Shirley close behind him. At the end of the first lap, Larsen had built up a lead of some twelve yards, taking the circuit in 68.8 seconds. Brasher, meanwhile had slid back to seventh place, though he looked to be running comfortably and at that stage there was nothing to be gained by noting the positions, save to wonder if the Norwegian had done a foolish thing by moving in front so far and so quickly. After another lap, the

Chris Brasher, second left, during the vital 'protest lap'. Extreme left is Eric Shirley of Great Britain, while Larsen of Norway, who won the bronze medal, leads Rozsnyoi of Hungary who took the silver.

distance between Larsen and the Russian and Hungarian challengers had been narrowed slightly. After two and a half laps — one kilometre — Larsen had clocked 2min 52.4sec. Brasher was still tucked in seventh place, still running easily.

At the halfway stage, Brasher still had the same number of runners ahead of him, though the pattern had changed. Larsen now led by less than five yards and Disley had moved up to fourth with Shirley dropping back a place. The fifth lap was now coming up and here there was excitement as Brasher decided to make his move onwards. He went past his immediate leaders and snuggled back into fourth position with Larsen, Rzhishchin and Rozsnyoi taking him round. There were now only two laps still to run and now the Russian's increasingly fast pace began to tell on the Norwegian. With a spurt, Rzhishchin was past Larsen and into the lead. The Russian reached the bell in 7min 39.1sec and now he found himself struggling to maintain his lead. More important for British hopes was the fact that Brasher was still in contention. Both Disley and Shirley were fading fast and now the man who looked more at home with a brief case and bowler than a running vest realised that all his country's hopes of its first individual track gold medal since 1932 lay firmly with him.

Now it was the Hungarian, Rozsnyoi, who took up the lead. Brasher and Larsen were also there and with just four obstacles remaining — three hurdles and the water jump — and this was becoming an epic race. They came to the first hurdle and Brasher now went inside Larsen who seemed to check his stride slightly before joining the other two safely on the far side of the barrier. Now Brasher went for gold, running hard down the back straight. It seemed a suicidal move and it was some few seconds before the Hungarian realised what was happening

and went after the Briton. Brasher negotiated the penultimate hurdle safely, then gathered up all his strength to take the water jump, and finally skimmed the last hurdle before making the tape some fifteen yards ahead of Rozsnyoi. Brasher had done it! Britain's first track gold medal winner since Tommy Hampson won the 800 metres in Los Angeles twenty-four years earlier. He had also done it in 8min 41.2sec — over four seconds faster than the 1952 Olympic record. But had he really won a gold? Just ten minutes after Brasher crossed the finishing line came that dreaded announcement.

Brasher went into the jury room and came out; in went Larsen and the Norwegian team manager then had their say. Finally the decision was announced. The IAAF declared that although Brasher and Larsen had come into contact, they were satisfied that it was purely accidental and that it had not influenced the outcome of the race. It has to be said that Larsen made no complaint, and Laufer went as far as to say that if he was awarded a medal by default, then he would refuse it. Only the Hungarians, who had not been invited to give evidence, felt less than pleased at the decision, though again, the runner himself voiced no complaints. It was three hours after the end of the race before Brasher knew for certain that he had accomplished something even Bannister and Chataway — both world record holders — had not attained — an Olympic gold medal. They were probably the longest hours of Chris Brasher's life, yet he dealt with them superbly. In the words of Jack Crump, 'Chris Brasher won two battles today, one on the track, one in the jury room. But his greatest victory came between the two. Others might have torn the place to pieces; but Brasher showed neither tantrums nor self pity.' The runner who nearly did not go to Melbourne came home on the gold standard, both as an athlete and as a man.

# HERB ELLIOTT'S GOLDEN DUBLIN MILE

Herb Elliott was an athletics phenomenon. From the time he started serious training in 1954, aged just sixteen, until his retirement in 1962, the Western Australian from Subiaco, near Perth, never lost a 1,500 metres or mile race. During his relatively short international career between 1957 and 1960 he ran no less than forty-six races over one or the other of those distances and was never beaten in any of them. Of all the great mile competitors over the years, Elliott has been called the greatest of them all, and with his kind of record to back up that assessment there is little room for argument. Consider, for instance, that Elliott broke four minutes for the mile on no less than seventeen occasions; or that he won both the 880 yards and the mile at the Commonwealth Games in 1958; or that in the 1960 Rome Olympics he won the gold medal in the 1,500 metres in world record time — and breasted the tape a staggering twenty metres ahead of his nearest rival. But it was a race in Dublin in August 1958, for which Herb Elliott is best remembered. It was billed as a 'Golden Mile' and sure enough, it turned out to be a twenty-two carat event.

Herb Elliott's glittering career began in 1954 and in that year, aged sixteen, he ran 4min 25.6sec for the mile — which included a 58.8 seconds lap. This was the year in which Roger Bannister became the first man to pass through the four-minute barrier for the mile, and although Elliott's time was hardly sensational, it did auger well for his future. In 1955, and still aged sixteen — his seventeenth birthday was in February that year — Elliott ran 4min 20.8sec for the mile, and also improved his 880 yards time from 1min 58.2sec to 1min 55.8sec, before lowering his mile best once more later that year. He ran the mile in 4min 20.4sec and this young man was now being hailed as a potential world record-breaker. Two years later Elliott was still on course for making that prediction come true. Now aged eighteen, he set world junior bests for the mile (4min 4.3sec), 1,500 metres (3min 47.8sec), two miles (9min 1sec) and three miles (14min 2.4sec). Before his twentieth birthday in February 1958, Herb Elliott ran his first sub-four minute mile. Later that year he achieved that Dublin 'gold'.

Until Elliott appeared on the international scene, the running of a mile in under four minutes was worthy of headlines. Even today it is still regarded as a somewhat special event, but it was Elliott, aided by his great coach, Percy Cerutty, who made the achievement more commonplace than sensational. That evening in Dublin Elliott 'pulled' four more runners through the magic barrier. The field for the mile race held in the Santry Stadium on 6 August 1958 was an exceptionally fine one. Besides Elliott there were the Olympic 1,500 metres champion, Ron Delaney of Ireland; Alby Thomas, another Australian and the world three-miles record-holder; Murray Halberg of New Zealand, the Commonwealth Games three-miles champion; and yet another fine Australian miler, Merv Lincoln. Twenty-four hours after this race, Thomas was to break the world two-miles record with a fine run of 8min 32sec; and Murray Halberg would set a world best performance of 18min 22.6sec for four miles. This mile field, then, was one of high pedigree; and Herb Elliott, still six months short of his twenty-first birthday, was going to prove himself the pick of the show.

The weather was disappointing for the meeting organisers and the low grey clouds which gusted across the Irish capital brought with them an occasional spattering of rain. Nevertheless, some twenty thousand spectators packed themselves around what was undoubtedly one of the finest tracks in Europe; and with no appreciable wind to buffet the runners, the conditions were just

about as near to perfect as the milers could have hoped. An attempt on the world record was obviously 'on'. Since Bannister broke the magic barrier in 1954, two runners had bettered his time. John Landy lowered the record to 3min 58sec later that year; then Britain's Derek Ibbotson ran 3min 57.2sec in 1957. Ibbotson's run had been typical of this popular, cheerful athlete. He faced the most formidable opposition imaginable on that July evening in 1957 and was their absolute master. Ron Delaney finished ten metres behind Ibbotson, with Stanislav Jungwirth of Czechoslovakia second — the previous week the Czech had broken the world 1,500 metres record — and Ken Wood fourth. All the first four past the post clocked sub-four minute miles and it was Ibbotson's record on which the Dublin runners now had their

sights firmly set. At this time Ibbotson's record was still unratified, but there were people who felt that 3min 55sec was the absolute human limit for running one mile. Herb Elliott was about to prove them wrong.

The race began with Alby Thomas taking an early lead and the Australian took the runners around the first lap in 56 seconds. It was still Thomas throughout the second lap — his time for the half-mile was 1min 58sec. But Herb Elliott was so determined to have that world record. As the runners entered the third lap, Elliott took over the lead. The Australian looked to be full of running and he could hardly have expected to be seriously challenged now. But there was to be a challenge and it came in the shape of fellow Australian, Merv Lincoln, the man who had so often found himself in Elliott's shadow. Lincoln took up the lead and led the way until they approached the bell. Elliott went into the last lap having run the first three-quarters of a mile in 2min 59sec, and now there was no stopping him. Elliott went smoothly into top gear and stormed away from the rest of the field. As he went into the home straight it was so obvious that he would break the world record by a wide margin. He went through the tape in 3min 54.5sec — a full 2.7 seconds inside Ibbotson's record — and there can have been no greater finish in the history of mile racing.

Elliott's second half-mile was run in 1min 56.5sec, which was more than four seconds faster than that stage of Bannister's first sub-four-minute mile four years earlier and of Ibbotson's record the previous year. The Australian had taken the other runners through the barrier too. Merv Lincoln was second in 3min 55.9sec, Ron Delaney third in 3min 57.5sec, and Murray Halberg fourth, also in 3min 57.5sec. All of them had beaten the existing approved world record set by John Landy. A fifth runner, Alby Thomas (3min 58.6sec) also ran faster than four minutes. Elliott's time had confounded the experts who claimed that it would be impossible to run inside 3min 55sec. Elliott was obviously drained as he crossed the line, having called on all his immense store of stamina to take him into another realm of mile running. He had, for a long time, shown that his style was to take the lead with about a lap and a half to go; and from the moment he regained the lead from Lincoln he gave the astounded spectators one of the most incredible displays of power running.

Elliott went on to other triumphs in 1958. He broke the world 1,500 metres record with 3min 36sec; won two gold medals at the Commonwealth Games in Cardiff; set a new Commonwealth Games record of 1min 47.3sec for the 880 yards; and in the space of just eight days ran 1,500 metres in 3min 36sec, a mile in 3min 58sec, a mile in 3min 55.4sec, and 1,500 metres in 3min 37.4sec. There was little wonder that Herb Elliott was now the hottest property in athletics and it was reported that he turned down an offer worth almost £90,000 to turn professional. Elliott had more to achieve as an amateur. In the 1960 Rome Olympics he took the 1,500 metres gold medal in a new world record time of 3min 35.6sec and finished an astonishing twenty metres ahead of the silver medallist, Michel Jazy of France. Elliott made the winning of a gold medal seem so very easy. He took the lead after 800 metres and surged majestically away to break his own world record. It was an extraordinary performance in an extraordinary career.

Elliott will always be remembered best for the 'Golden Mile' in Dublin, and his performance during that meeting overshadowed that of his fellow countryman, Alby Thomas, who had passed the four-minute barrier during that epic race and then on the following evening broke a world record himself, beating Herb Elliott in the process. Thomas had a particular liking for the Santry Stadium track. Less than one month previously he had broken the world three-miles record there, running it in 13min 10.8sec to lower the standard set by Inharos in Budapest three years previously. The evening following the mile, Thomas, Elliott and others — the Australians were the only visitors in the field of nine runners — set out on the two-mile trail. The Australians set a fast pace and they covered the first lap in 63 seconds. At the end of the second lap, Elliott led in 2min 10sec. Another 67 seconds lap followed and the order was still unchanged; at the halfway stage Elliott led Thomas in 4min 22sec. The fifth lap found Thomas in the lead and with a 61 second lap put himself well in line for a world record. At the beginning of the sixth lap Elliott regained the lead for a short while, but down the back straight Thomas went in front once more. The sixth lap ended with Thomas still in the lead having clocked 6min 30sec. There was now half a mile to run and the crowd now urged Thomas on. He opened up a commanding lead and reached the bell in 7min 31sec. Thomas was now unbeatable. He ran the last lap in 61 seconds to take the record in 8min 32sec, leaving Elliott some twenty yards behind.

Indeed, this was a good meeting for world record attempts. The same day, Murray Halberg, the New Zealander who was one of the previous day's sub-four-minute milers, set a world best performance of 18min 22.6sec for the four miles. Yet all these performances were overshadowed by the incredible Herb Elliott. He had led a field of fine athletes round what was described on the following day as 'the finest mile race ever run'. There have been quite a few races so called — and some have arguably deserved the title — but there can be no doubt that Herb Elliott, the young man from Perth, Western Australia, was one of, if not *the* greatest milers of all time.

# BAREFOOT IN THE DARK

The sweat glistened on the ebony skin of the man threading his way through the ruins of tombs and catacombs, his ghostly figure disappearing, then reappearing, through the shadows of the cypress trees. Behind him came another dark-skinned man, then still more men. The man in front was running barefoot around the monuments of Ancient Rome, his quickening pace eating up metre after metre of the Appian Way, built by Appius Claudius some three centuries before the birth of Christ. But this was no manhunt conducted by soldiers of the Roman Empire, though Italian soldiers did line the path of the runners, lighting up the gloom with torches which only heightened the dramatic effect of the occasion. For the barefooted black man at the head of this almost eerie procession of men making their way through the Roman darkness was a hitherto unknown Ethiopian who was about to burst on to the Olympic stage to become one of the best-known — and best-loved — athletes of all time. Abebe Bikila, private soldier in the Imperial Bodyguard of Emperor Haile Selassie, was about to win the 1960 Olympic Games marathon in a world record time.

Abebe Bikila arrived in Rome in September 1960 mindful of the fact that his countrymen had no love for the Italians. A quarter of a century before, Ethiopia, or Abyssinia, had been invaded by Mussolini's fascists intent on a twentieth-century Roman adventure. Bikila's parents had seen the Italians make yet another claim on their country, this time with all the paraphernalia of modern warfare — air power, mechanised equipment, even poison gas. In 1941, the Emperor was restored to the throne and peace eventually ensued. Yet a visit to the land of his country's former conquerors was still a painful experience for the tall, erect soldier who was so proud to serve Haile Selassie, the 'Lion of Africa'.

Bikila was fortunate in being coached by Onni Niskanen, a Swede of great ability and with a resounding belief that his charge would do well in the marathon race at Rome's Games. It was said that during his training for the 1960 Olympics, Bikila had run a marathon in a time of 2hr 21min 23sec, well inside the Olympic record set by Emil Zatopek in Helsinki in 1952. If that was correct then it was an astonishing performance and there were many who felt that the time was incorrect — or if it was correct, then the distance which Bikila had covered was well inside the official marathon distance. For a barefoot runner like Bikila, who set the most ferocious pace, it seemed that a marathon could not be negotiated in anything like that time. Despite his coach, Bikila's technique appeared to be that of an immature runner. Surely, he would not trouble the favourites for a gold medal in Rome?

This Olympic marathon set a precedent in that it was the first in modern times which neither started, nor finished, in the Olympic stadium. The organisers, with a proper sense of theatre, decided to use this ancient city as the backcloth to one of the most evocative events on the Olympic agenda. Over sixty athletes assemfed on the Capitoline Hill, in the Piazza del Campidoglio. Their task was to run 26 miles and 385 yards to the Arch of Constantine, near the Colosseum. On their journey they would pass most of the splendours of Ancient Rome. It was an imaginative piece of planning. The barefoot Ethiopian would ensure that its finale could not have been more fitting than if the organisers had stage-managed it. The gun barked out and the runners were off, at first sprawling in an almost unseemly rush to find their favourite and most comfortable position before settling down to work out their own individual plan for survival in what is one of the world's most gruelling sporting events. Many probably remembered

*Marathon runners pass the Colosseum at the start of the 1960 Olympic race.*

the great marathon races of the past before putting aside all thoughts but those designed to steer them safely along twenty-six miles of history.

The multi-coloured crocodile which was forming from the initial sea of bodies began to stretch out from the Forum and sort itself out along the spacious Via del Teatro di Marcello. The front runners swept past the Theatre of Marcellus towards the Circus Maxiumus where athletes of another age had fought against each other in the games of old. Now there were no chariot races, no gladitorial contests. Yet the determination, the battle for survival, was almost as strong. After about a quarter of an hour, the leading runners went through the 5-kilometre mark. There was Arthur Keily of Great Britain, one of a great family of athletes from the English industrial town of Derby. Keily had spent hours pounding the roads of his hometown, sometimes in the company of one or more of his brothers, at other times desperately

alone as he battled against the clock. There was the Moroccan, Allah Saoudi, and the Belgian, Aurele Van Den Driessche.

The runners now left the inner limits of Rome and could relax a little as they swallowed up the Via Cristoforo Colombo going south out of the city. Bikila was now about to work his way into third position behind Saoudi and Keily and he passed the monuments to the fascist regime as he went through the Esposizione Universale de Roma, and perhaps took a sideways look at the reminders of another Italy, an Italy which had raped his own country not so long before. The way out of Rome was uphill but this appeared to make no difference to the pace set by the leaders of the crocodile which had now become a snake, stretched right back along several hundred yards of Roman roadways. Keily was still in the lead and he passed the 15-kilometre mark in a couple of seconds over forty-eight minutes. The Belgian, Van Den Driessche, was second, while

73

Bikila had settled back into fourth spot with another Moroccan, Rhadi Ben Abdesselem, now in third, Allah Saoudi having dropped back slightly. The return to Rome along the Appian Way was coming up and it was here that Rhadi decided to make the break. On the Grande Raccordo Anulare, the little Moroccan streaked clear of the field and his rearguard could only look on in astonishment.

Even Bikila found himself some fifty yards behind the fast-disappearing leader, though the Ethiopian was the one man who had the ability to take up the challenge. Keily and Van Den Driessche, meanwhile, were left far behind and now the race entered a crucial stage as Bikila drew closer and closer to the speeding Rhadi. At the 20-kilometre stage, Rhadi clocked 1hr 2min 39sec, while back in the second bundle of runners, other dramatic changes were beginning to take place. Keily now found that the Russian, Sergei Popov, was coming up on his shoulder. Popov, the European champiom was the favourite to win this marathon. Now he was trying to find the superhuman effort needed to get back into contention with the two dark-skinned gentlemen who were apparently intent on staging a race of their own. In addition to Popov, Keily now felt the further pressure of the New Zealander, Barry Magee, and the battle for the other placings was now as hot as the struggle for gold.

In the ever-growing darkness, Rhadi and Bikila began the long descent of the Appian Way. Here it was that Italian soldiers lined the route with torches to light the way; and here it was that the ghostly procession began to weave through the ruins and the trees. Then the two front runners started to climb gently again towards the Porto San Sebastiano. On and up the road towards the Piazzale Numa Pompilio, past the Roman baths of Caracalla, into Via delle Terme di Caracalla, it was a splendid race with the Olympic record of Zatopek already seemingly perished, and the world record itself under direct threat. The forty kilometre post was passed in 2hr 8min 33sec, and then Bikila went in front. He swept into the Via di San Gregorio with a lead of over fifty yards

while the gallant Rhadi could only struggle and watch the Ethiopian sweep further away from him. At last Bikila saw the Arch of Constantine come into view. Ten thousand Romans and others had packed into the temporary stands erected for just this moment. They cheered and roared as the barefoot runner from the land of Haile Selassie breasted the tape in 2hr 15min 16.2sec. He was almost eight minutes inside Zatopek's record and had also broken the world best for the marathon. Little Rhadi took the silver medal some two hundred yards behind, while brave Kiwi, Barry Magee, was rewarded with the bronze.

The Olympic Games marathon gold medal had never been won twice by the same man,

*Abebe Bikila of Ethiopia acknowledges the cheers after running barefoot to the gold medal.*

and in October 1964, no one felt that this man from Africa, Abebe Bikila, could break that record in the Tokyo Games. Since the Roman triumph of four years earlier, Bikila had made few appearances and in the Boston marathon of 1963 — one of his rare races outside his native land — he had finished fifth. In addition he had suffered the removal of his appendix only five weeks before the Tokyo race. No, it seemed that Bikila would be unable to do it, even though this time he wore shoes and socks. Ben Boubaker of Tunisia led the early field and at the 5-kilometre mark it was the great Australian, Ron Clarke, who took over with Jim Hogan (Ireland), Ron Hill (Great Britain) and Jeff Julian (New Zealand) following him. Boubaker and his fellow Tunisian, Hannachi, were behind all these.

But Bikila was not going to be outdone, At 10 kilometres — taken in 30min 14sec — the Ethiopian had moved up on Clarke and Hogan. That stage had been reached almost a minute faster than the same stage in Rome, and after forty-five minutes the front runners passed the 15-kilometre stage. Now Bikila began to forge ahead. He punished Clarke and Hogan mercilessly and at 20 kilometres he was well clear in a time of 1hr 58sec. About 35 kilometres, Hogan fell away, joining Clarke who had given up the ghost some considerable time before. Bikila was on his way to yet another world record marathon. He entered the stadium to rapturous applause and hit the tape in 2hr 12min 11.2sec. It was an effort which would have crippled many athletes. Bikila merely did a few exercises to keep the crowd amused until their home favourite, Kokichi Tsuburaya, entered the stadium to contest the silver medal with Basil Heatley, the Briton who had made such valiant strides over the last few miles. The Japanese led by ten yards, but Heatley closed up and passed the line in front of him, taking the silver medal just four minutes and eight seconds behind Bikila.

Abebe Bikila had done what we all thought was impossible. Now he turned his thoughts to 1968 and the Mexico Games where he knew that the rarified atmosphere was much the same as the conditions in Addis Ababa where he trained. The man who had risen from private soldier to lieutenant in the Imperial Guard felt that this would be the easiest of all his marathon attempts. It was his goal to go for what really was an impossible treble. Sadly, a leg injury ruled out any chance he had, and we shall never know if Abebe Bikila could have accomplished that incredible feat. He started the Mexico race but was forced to drop out after about seventeen kilometres. Ethiopia did achieve a third marathon gold medal, however, when Mamo Wolde, who had the silver medal in the 10,000 metres, took Bikila's place with honour. Abebe Bikila was ever the competitor and he now looked forward to Munich in 1972. Here fate took a final cruel hand. In March 1969, Bikila was badly injured in a motor accident which left him with hideous spinal injuries and permanently paralysed legs. The man who had won so much honour with his running, could now not so much as walk across a room. In October 1973, at the age of forty-one, he died after suffering a brain haemorrhage. That same month, Paavo Nurmi, too, died aged seventy-six. The world mourned the loss of two great athletes. They remembered, too, that evening in Rome when the ghostly figure of Abebe Bikila flitted barefoot through the dark in search of gold.

# LYNN AND MARY - LONG JUMP DOUBLE ACT

The rain sheeted down over the Tokyo Olympic stadium, the wind gusted and blustered, and the biting cold ate into the bones. It reminded Lynn Davies of home back in Nantymoel, Glamorgan, where the days often seemed so grey and wet and cold. Yet this flash of his Welsh homeland, where he had been brought up the son of a coal-miner, did little to calm his nerves. He had slept little the previous night; now the churning of his stomach brought the tension still tighter. He peeled off his tracksuit and considered the position. Here he was, lying third in the 1964 Olympic long jump final behind the Russian, Igor Ter-Ovanesyan, and the American, Ralph Boston with the task now of leaping beyond Boston's 7.88 metres (25ft 10.25in) in a last-ditch attempt to take the second long jump gold medal of these Games for Britain. If he did, he would become the first Welshman ever to win a gold medal; and the first British male to win an Olympic field event gold medal since 1908. All these thoughts flooded through Davies's mind as he watched the red flag go up to signal that Boston's fifth jump was a foul. Then the Welshman looked at the flag which was flying high over the stadium, almost being torn from its mast by the swirling wind; as he looked up to the sky he saw the flag drop suddenly against its pole — and he knew that, for a few seconds at least, the wind had dropped. It was enough. Davies moved on to the approach and was immediately into his run, legs pumping hard down the churned-up run. He hit the board and took off, hitchkicking his way towards the mark left by Boston. One, two, two and a half . . . Davies thumped back into the clammy sand. It was a good one.

*Lynn Davies, one half of Britain's long jump double act.*

Now came the wait. The jump was measured, the red flag had stayed down, and all that remained was for the electronic scoreboard to announce the distance. In all, that operation took almost four minutes. Davies chatted nervously with his coach,

Ron Pickering, asking him — had they really done enough to take the gold? Then the measurement flashed up. As soon as an 'eight' appeared Davies knew he was almost there. It was 8.07 metres (26ft 5.75in) — a new British record, and surely a winning Olympic jump?

These were great Games for Britain. Already the Olympic women's long jump gold medal was in British hands. Ken Matthews, the walker, had won the 20,000 kilometres in record time; the women's pentathlon also had a silver medal winner from Britain; Ann Packer had taken the silver in the 400 metres, and silvers had also gone to steeplechaser Maurice Herriott, swimmer Bobby McGregor, weightlifter Louis Martin, and the coxless fours also took a silver at Toda. Then Paul Nihill won the silver in the 50 kilometres walk; and finally there was Lynn Davies, the Welshman they called 'Lynn the Leap' and his gold medal. Yes, they were great Games for the British contingent and yet many other names fade into the background behind Davies and the girl who took the women's long jump to snatch a gold double for Britain. Consider that no British athlete had won a long jump title for Britain before 1964, and that you had to go back well over half a century for the last British gold medal in the field events, and you will realise that the double achieved by Davies and that girl — Mary Rand — was not just a mild coincidence, it was quite a sensation.

Mary Rand had been to the Olympics before. In 1960, as twenty-year-old Mary Bignal, she had been favourite for a medal. The pretty girl with the cropped blonde hair had led the qualifiers in Rome, but in the final she had flopped badly and finished ninth. Now, four years later, Mary Bignal was Mary Rand, married to the Olympic sculler, Sydney Rand, and with a training jump quite a way over the 1960 Olympic record. Right from the qualifying competition in Tokyo she took the lead and soared past the new Olympic record which had been set just a few jumps earlier by the German girl, Helga Hoffmann. That Olympic record-breaking jump of Mary Rand's measured 6.52 metres (21ft 4.75in). There was no doubt that she would qualify and the period while others tried to reach the final was one of the few relaxing moments that Mary Rand enjoyed on that Wednesday of 14 October 1964. Mary's first jump had seen her through. Now she waited for the others to join her.

Shortly after three o'clock that afternoon the girls came back for the final and Mary Rand was straight into the thick of the action, clearing her Olympic record of that morning by almost three inches with a jump of 6.59 metres (21ft 7.5in). None of the other girls managed to get beyond twenty-one feet and the competition moved into the second round. Mary Rand jumped 6.56 metres (21ft 6.25in) against the wind and was then surprised when the Polish sprinter, Irena Kirszenstein, jumped a personal best of 6.43 metres (21ft 1.25in) to add a little pressure. There were the others to consider, too, including the world record-holder, Tatyana Shchelkanova, and the American girl, Willye White. The wind was now gusting strongly, though hindering rather than helping the jumpers, and Mary Rand jumped again, this time 6.57 metres (21ft 6.75in). Then Kirszenstein went within one and a quarter inches of the British girl's mark, followed by Shchelkanova with a jump also over the twenty-one feet mark. Mary Rand responded magnificently. Her next jump took her to 6.63 metres (21ft 9in) and yet another Olympic record. The Pole failed to clear twenty feet and was obviously feeling the pressure; but then she went to 6.60 metres (21ft 7.75in) which was a personal best. Mary Rand now had the competition within her grasp, but she made absolutely sure in the most astonishing fashion. Running into the wind, remember, she hit the board and soared to 6.76 metres (22ft 2.25in). It was the first time that a woman had ever jumped over twenty-two feet. As if it mattered, both Russian and Pole saw the red flag raised against them on their last jumps and the gold was Mary's, though not before she had jumped well over twenty-one feet in her last attempt.

Her biggest thrill though was not the Olympic gold medal, much as that meant to her, but the world record. Athletes have been known to become Olympic champions through circumstances beyond their immediate control — accidents or loss of form of other challengers — but there is no arguing with a world record. Mary Rand's Olympics were far from over just yet. She still had the pentathlon to contend, and as the British champion and record-holder with the most number of points — 4,466, — under the scoring system then being used, she had every reason to feel confident that she would be in the medals once more.

Mary Rand and the other Mary — Mary Peters — who would bring so much pride and heart back to Ulster sport in another Olympics, knew that their main rivals in the 1964 pentathlon would come from the two Russian girls, Bystrova and Press. In the 80 metres hurdles both Russians clocked 10.7

seconds, with Mary Rand recording 10.9 and Mary Peters 11.00 seconds. In the shot Mary Rand fell way behind with a throw of only 10.05 metres (36ft 3in) to take less than 800 points while the two Russians and Mary Peters, who finished second in that event, each rattled up more than 1,000. The high jump found Mary Rand in better heart, for this was a much better event for her than the shot. She won it with a personal-best of 1.72 metres (5ft 7.75in) which left her in fourth place behind the two Russians and her fellow Briton. Mary Peters was just one point behind Bystrova; Mary Rand, with 2,917 points, was 328 behind the leader, Press. There were now just two events left, the long jump and the 200 metres. The long jump should not have caused the world champion any problems and, indeed, it did not. Mary Rand came first with 6.55 metres (21ft 5.75in) which took her to second place having earned her 1,111 points. In the 200 metres she won the race in 24.2 seconds to

*Mary Rand, the other half of the great duo.*

earn another 1,000-plus score. It was a great performance from the British girl but not great enough. Irina Press did 24.7 seconds for the 200 metres and that was enough to ease her into the gold medal spot. But Mary Rand took the silver medal and became only the second woman to pass the 5,000 points total. Press was first with 5,246 points, Rand second with 5,035. Mary Peters failed to take the bronze — but her turn would come.

So, Mary Rand and the other Britons were acquitting themselves well. Now all eyes turned to Lynn Davies in the long jump, though the thought of a golden double for Great Britain was, in truth, somewhat remote. It was Davies's first Olympic Games so, unlike Mary Rand, he had no experience on which to draw. It showed immediately in the qualifying competition when the Welshman failed to make the qualifying mark with his first leap, and then heard the groans as the red flag was raised in his wake on the second attempt. It has to be underlined that the weather was quite appalling, though if it suited anybody, then it suited the miner's son from Nantymoel rather better than any of the others. Davies measured his third run, realised that he had been two feet out, and went through more comfortably to 7.78 metres (25ft 6.5in).

It was a good jump, bettered only by the world record holder, Ralph Boston, who leapt over eight metres that morning, and taking into account the weather, was one of the better attempts. A measure of the difficult conditions was the fact that only five athletes managed to pass the qualifying distance of 7.60 metres (24ft 11.25in) so that the Olympic officials had no option but to include the best seven 'failures' to make up the number of jumpers for the final. After the first round of that final, Igor Ter-Ovanesyan, the Russian who took the bronze medal in Rome and who was the current European champion, led the way with Boston in second place and Wariboko West, of Nigeria, in third spot. Davies lay fourth after his first jump of 7.45 metres (24ft 5.25in). It was a disappointing effort from the man who, a few days before the Olympic Games, had

jumped over twenty-six feet during practice. The second jump was even more morale-shattering when Davies fouled on take-off. His only consolation was that the Russian had also been red-flagged and was now in second place behind Boston.

With his third jump Davies improved to 7.59 metres (24ft 10.75in) and went into third place, bettering that still further on his fourth attempt with 7.78 metres (25ft 6.25in). Boston, meanwhile, had jumped 7.88 metres (25ft 10.25in) in that fourth round and as the athletes prepared themselves for their fifth jumps, they each knew that this was the mark they now had to beat. That was the point at which Boston fouled and Davies looked up at that momentarily limp flag, knowing that this was his one chance of giving Britain its golden double. Davies took that chance and went through to 8.07 metres (26ft 5.75in). It must surely be good enough to take the gold? Both Davies and Pickering thought that it was — but there was still another round of jumps to go after the Russian's fifth jump saw him fail to better Davies, though his 7.99 metres (26ft 2.5in) was still a fine performance considering that the flag was now fluttering strongly once more as the wind got up again.

That jump put the Russian back in second place ahead of the world champion. Now Ralph Boston prepared for his final jump knowing that the gold medal was slipping away from him. Here was a man capable of going beyond twenty-seven feet. A jump of those proportions would mean the kiss of death for Davies. Boston's black skin glistened — was it rain or was it the nervous perspiration of a man who knows that the eyes of the world are upon him? Whatever, Boston pounded down the approach hit the board — the red flag stayed down — and 'bicycled' through the air. The jump was a good one — but good enough? Again there were the agonising moments while the measurement was taken. The figure eight flashed up, then a zero . . . then a three. Boston had failed to overtake the Welshman. Now Davies prepared for his final leap. It was 7.74 metres (25ft 4.75in) and obviously the incredible

*Mary Rand, of L.O.A.C. wins the senior 100 yards event in 10.9 seconds, at the Southern Counties Women's AAA Championships in 1964.*

pressure had drained the front man's final spark. All that remained was for the Russian to attack. But Ter-Ovanesyan hit the damp sand far short of his best and Davies had the gold medal.

Lynn Davies still had the 4 x 100 metres relay and he helped Britain to a place in the final, though here, despite setting a new British record, the men finished last of eight. For Mary Rand it was a happier ending when she was part of the British team which took the bronze in the relay behind Poland and America, thus giving Mary a full set of Olympic medals. For Mary, though, her finest hour had been in that long jump pit. In the Commonwealth Games, in Jamaica, in 1966, she took the gold, but then finished eleventh in the European Championships

later that year and was forced out of the 1968 Olympic Games through injury. For Lynn Davies, things actually got better with a gold in Jamaica and in the European Championships. Those who said the Welshman had been lucky with the wind speed in Mexico did him a great disservice, forgetting the hours of hard training he had put in under coach Ron Pickering. Lynn Davies was a natural long jumper. It was only in Mexico in 1968, when Bob Beamon astonished the world with a superhuman leap of over twenty-nine feet, that even Lynn Davies realised there was little point in going on. Athletes need new peaks to scale; Davies felt that Beamon had left him — and the rest of the world — an impossible target.

# THE FLYING KIWI

On the afternoon of 10 October 1964, a young Japanese athlete, Yoshinoro Sakai, ran the final lap of the Olympic torch relay and lit the flame which symbolised the friendship of sportsmen and women around the world. It was a moving and immensely significant part of the opening ceremony of the Eighteenth Olympiad. Less than twenty years before, Yoshinoro Sakai had been born under the shadow of the atomic bomb which burst over the Japanese city of Hiroshima. Now his act in lighting the Olympic flame in Tokyo was perhaps the final gesture which confirmed that the world now accepted Japan as an equal partner. Japan had originally been scheduled to host the 1940 Olympic Games, Games which, of course, never took place. When the world was ready to reassume some kind of normality in 1948 with the London Olympic Games, it was not ready to admit Japan, nor Germany for that matter, to the jamboree. Four years later, in Helsinki in 1952, Japanese athletes had competed; now the world chose to forgive, if not to forget, and nineteen years after the mushroom clouds rose over Hiroshima and Nagasaki, nearly two decades after the prisoners of war staggered half-starved from the camps of the Far East, Japan assumed the final mantle of respectability in playing host to the Olympic Games.

In the stadium on that historic day in 1964 was a young New Zealander, Peter Snell, a member of his country's team and already holder of a gold medal from the 1960 Rome Olympics. Snell was now twenty-five years old. He was in Tokyo to attempt two things — to retain his 800 metres title, and to take the gold medal in the 1,500 metres, though amazingly he had never run a competitive race over that distance before arriving in Japan. Snell had gone to the Rome Olympics as a complete unknown outside his own corner of the world; he came to Tokyo as a champion expected to do what very few New Zealanders had done before him, for since Jack Lovelock won an epic 1,500 metres race in Berlin in 1936 only one Kiwi had taken a gold track medal, Snell himself, in Rome.

Snell had prepared for Rome and the 800 metres with a series of punishing, desperate runs around the Auckland hills. It seems a strange way for an 800-metres runner to train, but his coach, Arthur Lydiard, believed in building up his pupil's stamina. So it was that Peter Snell found himself on the body-wracking grind along with runners like Barry Magee, the marathon runner, and other Kiwi long distance men. It was a schedule that was designed to build, not only stamina, but also the character and sheer guts needed to compete in the fiercely competitive arena of international athletics. Snell certainly benefited from the attentions of Lydiard, and his first real success came with the setting of a New Zealand national record for the half mile in 1min 49.2sec.

This was the background to Snell's Rome Olympic Games. The Italian capital was enduring its hottest spell of weather for a decade when Peter Snell and his team mates flew in from the other side of the world. The first two rounds of the 800 metres were scheduled for the last day of August and it was now that Snell really appreciated the energy-building runs which Lydiard had pushed him through. In his first round heat Snell was an easy winner and, more important, had clocked a personal-best time of 1min 48.1sec. It was the fastest time of the first round of heats and in the second round the New Zealander was happy to qualify with second place and a time of 1min 48.6sec. The semi-finals were staged the next day and again Snell went through, again winning in his fastest-ever time, 1min 47.2sec. The Olympic record had already been broken by the Jamaican, George Kerr, but these personal times meant a great deal to the New Zealander who began to realise that his country's first

81

*Peter Snell wins the 1964 Olympic 800 metres final with Crothers of Canada second and Kiprugut third.*

run that was the order but now Snell summoned up all his reserves and went past the Belgian to take the gold in 1min 46.3sec, a new Olympic record.

What a day this had been for New Zealand. Before it was over, Murray Halberg, the man who had joined Peter Snell on so many of those gruelling runs around the Auckland hills, made it a double success for the Kiwis by winning the gold medal in the 5,000 metres, winning that race by some twenty-five metres from the silver medallist. Snell was now a world figure in athletics. In July 1961 he was a member of the New Zealand team which took the 4 x 1 mile relay world record in Dublin; and in January 1962, at Wanganui, he shook the world with a record run in the mile. Not only did Snell break four minutes for the first time, the man in the black vest also went straight into the record book with 3min 54.4sec. It was one-tenth of a second inside Herb Elliott's world record — and it had been achieved on a grass track! Elliott, gold medallist in the Rome 1,500 metres, had retired the previous year, aged just twenty-two, because he felt that there were no more peaks left to conquer. Now his fellow Australiasian, Peter Snell, had offered down a gauntlet. The whole athletics world wanted Elliott to pick it up, but he did not. This was as much to the disappointment of Snell as to anyone else. If Elliott had chosen to race again, then Snell could have proved, or disproved the inevitable, and impossible, comparisons which people made between the New Zealander and the Australian.

Before the Tokyo Olympics, Peter Snell had more world-beating feats up his sleeve. On 3 February 1962, at Lancaster Park, Christchurch, he took part in an 880 yards race. At the halfway stage, Snell found that he was so far in front that his only challenger now was the clock, and how magnificently he responded to that challenge. He passed 800 metres in 1min 44.3sec — 1.4 seconds inside the world record — and breasted the tape in 1min 45.1sec — 1.7 seconds inside that world record. Three world records in the space of eight days made Peter Snell a living legend in the world of athletics. The

track gold medal for almost a quarter of a century was a real prospect. The final of the 800 metres was on 2 September and from the start, the Swiss runner, Waegli, went away fast, but he had just beaten the gun and the runners were recalled in a moment of high tension. The second time the gun fired all was well and again the Swiss went away first with the German Paul Schmidt, Kerr, Snell and the world-record holder, Roger Moens of Belgium. With three-quarters of the race over, Waegli was still in front at 1min 19.1sec. Moens had moved up to second spot with Snell hard on his heels. The runners came round the final bend and into the straight with Moens now the leader, Snell closing hard. With twenty metres to offers came flooding in and he flew to America and raced against the top athletes there before going on to Perth and the 1962 Commonwealth Games and gold medals in the 880 yards and the mile. Tokyo now loomed large and we asked outselves if this magnificent New Zealander could win a golden double in the metric equivalents.

But Peter Snell had other distractions. He had failed his examinations as a quantity surveyor — an inevitable price paid for his total dedication to running — and he was to be married, a step which brought all the attendant worries of the breadwinner. But Peter Snell had one great thing going for him — he was world famous. The Rothmans tobacco company gave him a job and he arrived in Tokyo somewhat more settled in his mind. His first job was to qualify for the 800 metres final, and he was drawn to run in the fourth heat on a wet and dull October day. His immediate rival was the American, Jerry Siebert, and the heavy track meant that there would be no fast time. Snell took the heat in 1min 49sec, destroying the American over the last twenty metres, and we began to look on him as the ultimate champion once more. The next day saw the semi-finals and again Snell led the way, this time in 1min 46.9sec; the second semi-final provided a new Olympic record — 1min 46.1sec run by George Kerr; and the third and final race found a winner in the Canadian, Bill Crothers. That left the final between Peter Snell and a second gold medal. More than 80,000 spectators were there to witness it and Snell did not let them down. Though the Kenyan, Wilson Kiprugut, took the early lead, the New Zealander overcame a potentially dangerous situation at the bell, when it looked for a heart-stopping moment as if he had been boxed in, and took the gold in 1min 45.1sec. He took back his Olympic record and was followed home by Crothers, and then Kiprugut.

Peter Snell had shown in those last few metres, just what a great champion he was; his final, telling burst over the final stretch had left his opponents for dead. All thoughts now turned to the 1,500 metres; could Peter Snell accomplish the double? The pressure on the New Zealander was immense, especially since he had never run a competitive race over this distance. In the heats he was happy to qualify by finishing in fourth place behind the winner, Kipchoge Keino, who had the previous day qualified for the 5,000 metres in a fast heat won by Ron Clarke. Doubts that Snell might have over-reached himself quickly disappeared in the 1,500 metes semi-final when he took the race with comfort, clocking 3min 38.8sec. It now gave rise to the thought that Peter Snell might break through Herb Elliott's world and Olympic barrier of 3min 35.6sec. We should soon know.

The 1,500 metres final was set for a Wednesday, 21 October, and in it New Zealand had two runners, Snell and John Llewellyn-Davies, a Londoner by birth who had clocked better times than Snell during the pre-Olympic races. Britain had John Whetton and Alan Simpson; France were represented by Michel Bernard and Jean Wadoux; Poland had Witold Baran; Czechoslovakia, Josef Odlozil; and the American, Dyrol Burleson made up the field. The Frenchman, Bernard, went away first, just as he had done in Snell's semi-final. As the runners entered the second lap, Bernard found that he had done too much and John Whetton, no doubt much to his dismay, found himself leading the field. Then he too was overhauled, this time by Llewellyn-Davies who went in front just about halfway round. The 800 metres came up in 2min 0.5sec with Llewellyn-Davies, Whetton, Snell, Baran, Simpson, Burleson, Bernard, Odlozil and Wadoux stretched out behind each other in that order. At the bell it was still the New Zealander, though now with Baran and Snell behind him and Whetton falling back. Round they went for the last time and everyone seemed to be waiting for Peter Snell to make his move.

There were 200 metres to go when Snell made that move. No one took up his challenge and he went through the tape in 3min 38.1sec. It was well outside Herb Elliott's record but New Zealand cared not. There

*The golden double as Snell takes the 1,500 metres gold.*

was still the battle for the silver with the Kiwis still very much in contention. Llewellyn-Davies and Odlozil had both passed Simpson and both came across the line together so that only a photograph could separate them. The all-seeing eye of the camera gave the silver to the Czech, New Zealand picked up the bronze and there only remained the imponderable of whether Snell could have beaten Elliott's record if there had been someone to push him over those last 200 metres. As it was he covered them in 25.4 seconds, but no one stayed at his elbow to shove him past Elliott's time. That was almost the end of Peter Snell. One month later he broke the world record for 1,000 metres in New Zealand, then shaved another three-tenths of a second off his mile record. But Peter Snell's heart seemed to have gone out of his running and when the young star, Jim Ryun, beat him in the United States in 1965, Snell retired with so many questions still unanswered.

# RON CLARKE - UNCROWNED KING OF THE TRACK

At the opening ceremony of the 1956 Olympic Games in Melbourne, Australia, a young man who was born in that graceful city nineteen years earlier was awarded the honour of carrying the Olympic torch. Around a decade later, that same young man was carrying all before him in the world of distance running, breaking and re-breaking world records from two miles to 20,000 metres and at one stage having no less than seventeen world records to his credit. Yet he flopped in both the Olympic Games and the Commonwealth Games in the 1960s, and never won a major international title. On a July evening in 1965, however, this young Australian ran a race at London's White City Stadium which catapulted him into a new age. Ron Clarke, the man they called a 'King without a Crown', became the first man to run three miles in under thirteen minutes. It was an epic performance and yet another display of world-shattering running which made him one of the greatest distance runners of all time.

Ron Clarke was born in Melbourne in February 1937. Early in 1956, at the age of eighteen, he was earmarked as Australia's new 'wonder boy' of athletics. He set new junior world bests for the mile (4min 6.8sec), two miles (9min 1.8sec) and 1,500 metres (3min 49.8sec) and although even that was not good enough to earn the young Clarke a place in Australia's team for the Olympic Games to be held in his native city later that year, it did earn him recognition as a star of the future and, with it, the great honour of being the local boy who carried that Olympic flame to its final destination in the great Melbourne Cricket Ground which hosted the main events of this Olympiad. Strangely,

though, Ron Clarke then slipped from the scene and it was not until five years later that he made a 'come-back'. It was in December 1963 that Clarke broke his first 10,000 metres world record, his 28min 15.6sec beating the record of 28min 18.2sec set by Pyotr Bolotnikov in August 1962. Clarke's first 5,000 metres record came in January 1965 when he ran that distance in 13min 34.8sec to beat the old time of 13min 35sec set by Vladimir Kuts in October 1957. Before his career was ended, Clarke lowered both records still further, ultimately reaching 27min 39.4sec for the 10,000 metres, and 13min 16.6sec for the 5,000 metres.

Clarke went to the 1964 Olympic Games in Tokyo as the hot favourite to win the 10,000 metres for, after all, he was the world record-holder. Through the first few laps, Clarke led the thirty-eight strong field. By the halfway stage he had lost most of his challengers, but with one lap to go there were at least two runners who he just could not shake off. Tunisia's Mohamed Gammoudi and America's Billy Mills were still pressing him hard. As the front runners moved out to pass those being lapped, Clarke was still in the lead, but with Mills now breathing hard down his neck. But now both men were passed by Gammoudi and almost before Clarke and Mills realised what was happening, the North African had opened up a ten-yard lead with some 250 yards still to run. Gammoudi held that lead until there were just fifty yards left to run. Then Clarke came back again, only to be passed by Mills who went on to win the first United States gold medal in the longer track events. The Tunisian held on to the silver medal placing while Ron Clarke, everyone's favourite for the gold, had to be content with bronze. In the 5,000 metres, Clarke did not even have the consolation of a bronze medal. Again he made much of the pace but when it came to the bell he lacked the fast finish required and America's Bob Schul took the gold with a last 400 metres of 54.8 seconds. Ron Clarke finished in ninth place. The man who was to break the world record the following year had once again failed to earn himself a title. 85

*Ron Clarke salutes the cameraman.*

It was the same in the 1966 Commonwealth Games when Clarke added two more silver medals to the one he had collected in the three miles in the 1962 Commonwealth Games. The 1968 Olympic Games in Mexico City found him unable to come to terms with the high altitude; and in the 1970 Commonwealth Games he had to be content with yet another silver medal in the 10,000 metres. So, Clarke was apparently incapable of establishing himself as a major championship medal winner. Yet he was a breaker of world records and earned himself a series of brilliant victories against top-class opposition — but in races that did not carry the stamp of world-class competition. One of these victories over the stop-watch came at London's White City in July 1965 during the AAA Championships. It was one of Ron Clarke's most memorable runs.

The White City crowd were longing for their glimpse of the Australian who was on a European tour and who was scheduled for an attempt on the one-hour record of 12 miles 960 yards the following day, and to race over 10,000 metres in Oslo four days later, and over 5,000 metres in Paris two days after that. In an age when it is felt that athletes no longer run 'just for fun', we can look back and marvel at Ron Clarke who quite obviously just loved to run. He once said, 'To me, training is just like going for a walk.' On this evening in 1965, Clarke was twenty-eight years old, married with a family and was employed as a company secretary. He trained, it is recorded, three times each day, fitting that in between business and domestic commitments. He stood just under six feet tall, weighed around twelve stones, and his low-arm action and 'laid-back' style was hugely reminiscent of the runners of another era — the 1920s. His only weakness, so far as the commentators of the day could make out, was that he found it somewhat difficult to change gear and he was trying so hard to improve on his basic speed. Nevertheless, this smooth-running, easy-paced athlete with an absolutely perfect rhythmic stride was the uncrowned king of the day, so far as the long distance track was concerned.

The three-miles race was scheduled for a Saturday and right from the gun Clarke set out to destroy the rest of the field with his remorseless attack. For lap after lap during the first five circuits of the White City track, first one runner, then another, and then another, fell behind until Clarke had the race all but to himself, only the open road stretched out in front of him; his only challenger now appeared to be the even more remorseless hands of the stop-watch, ticking away the seconds as Clarke strove hard, not to simply win the race, but to beat his own world record. Yet there was still one runner who refused to concede. The incredibly brave American Lindgren, nineteen years old and skinny with it, who kept in touch when all the others had but given up the ghost. On the last bend of the ninth lap, Clarke suddenly slowed his pace and seemed to be inviting the American teenager to assume the lead. It was so reminiscent of that moment in the 1956 10,000 metres Olympic Games race when Vladimir Kuts had played a similar game with Britain's Gordon Pirie. Clarke's ploy, like that of the Russian master before him, worked. At that stage Lindgren was two yards down; at the next back straight he was twelve yards adrift and the last human challenger to Clarke was done for, though he still managed to get home in an American record time.

Clarke, meanwhile, was haring for the tape and the timekeepers at least realised that the world's first sub-thirteen minute three miles was a near-certainty. Clarke went through and the watch hands froze to confirm the time — 12min 52.4sec. It was an astonishing piece of running. Ron Clarke had bettered his own world record by a clear eight seconds. He had destroyed almost all the opposition after five laps; crushed the challenge of the young American, Lindgren after nine; and then won a battle against the stopwatch to become the first man to break thirteen minutes for the distance. Clarke had been worried about the challenge of Lindgren and the Briton, Wiggs, and from the third lap onwards he had employed a soul-destroying pace. His lap times make fascinating reading: 1st, 61.8sec; 2nd, 2min 4sec; 3rd, 3min 11sec; 4th, 4min 15.4sec; 5th, 5min 20.4sec; 6th, 6min 26sec; 7th, 7min 31.4sec; 8th, 8min 36.4sec; 9th 9min 42.8sec; 10th, 10min 46.8sec; 11th, 11min 51.4sec; and a final lap of 61 seconds which had the entire White City crowd on their feet, urging the Australian on to yet another landmark. Lindgren apart, only the Hungarian, Mecser, tried to stay with Clarke's blistering pace. The race was a fast one for almost every runner and Graham, though he was well out of contention from very early on, still managed to run two seconds faster than he had ever before achieved; even the thirty-year-old Wilkinson who finished in fifth place still managed to clip thirty seconds off his personal best with 13min 17.4sec. For Wiggs it was a different story and after making a desperate effort to stay in contention for the first mile, fell right away.

There have been few greater runners than Ron Clarke. He set world records for 3 miles, 6 miles, 10 miles, 5,000 metres, 10,000 metres, 20,000 metres and 1 hour. Only the great Paavo Nurmi could match that — and even he did not hold all those records simultaneously as Clarke did for a spell, also adding the two miles record to his list of achievements later on. Clarke's bid for the one-hour record on the day following his epic three miles race in July 1965 had to be called off when heavy rain flooded the Withdean Stadium track at Brighton where he was due to attempt another breathtaking feat. Instead, he chose to speak to a group of schoolchildren who were to represent Sussex in the English Schools Championships the following weekend. He stood under an umbrella and told the bunch of starry-eyed youngsters about his own philosophy on running. Truly, they could not have had a greater teacher.

# JOHN WALKER BREAKS A NEW MILE BARRIER

There is a danger, in selecting classic moments of athletics, of concentrating too heavily on one particular event — the mile. Yet there have been so many great mile races that it is impossible to avoid including more than just Bannister's first sub-four minute epic, indeed, it is not desirable to exclude other miles simply for the sake of balancing the picture with other events. In August 1975, for instance, a young New Zealander won a mile race in Gothenburg, Sweden. He won it in the remarkable time of under 3min 50sec — the first man to do so — and confirmed his status along with the other two great Kiwi milers who spring readily to mind, Jack Lovelock and Peter Snell.

John Walker was born in Papukura on 12 January 1952. His first memorable race was in the 1974 Commonwealth Games in his native New Zealand when he faced Filbert Bayi in the 1,500 metres. Bayi led from start to finish, covering the distance in 3min 32.2sec for a new world record. Walker may not have won but he was only two metres adrift at the tape and his own time of 3min 32.5sec also beat Jim Ryun's previous record. Later that year, in Helsinki, the two met again over the distance and this time Bayi 'blew up' after covering the first 1,200 metres in 2min 50.4sec, leaving Walker to gain his revenge with a victory gained in 3min 33.4sec. Like Lovelock and Snell before him, Walker achieved two of the greatest feats in athletics — the Olympic 1,500 metres title and the world record for the mile. His world record came in August 1975, in Sweden, just two weeks after narrowly missing Bayi's 1,500 metres record with 3min 32.4sec. The tall, muscular 23-year-old had passed the 1,200 metres mark in 2min 50.9sec, just half a second slower than the schedule which had caused Bayi's demise in Finland the previous year.

Bayi's 1,500 metres record was reckoned to be worth a 3min 50sec mile — the Tanzanian's world mile record, set in May of that year, was 3min 51sec — and already that summer Walker had run 3min 52sec. Filbert Bayi was not running in this race in Gothenburg — he had malaria — and Walker's one great ambition was to wrest at least one of the world records from his greatest rival. The New Zealander had a reputation of being a pleasant sort of a fellow. In his native land it appeared that they called him 'Fleet Street Walker' because of his complete lack of inhibition about talking to the Press. There could not have been a more popular man in the stadium that evening in 1975.

From the gun, Walker was led through the first 440 yards by the home favourite. Govan Savemark, who took the New Zealander through in 55.8 seconds. Savemark continued to dictate the pace for the second quarter, and the half-mile was reached in 1min 55.1sec. Still the race was being run to absolute perfection, but now Walker was on his own. The third quarter was covered in 57.9 seconds, giving a time for the three-quarter mile of 2min 53sec. There was no stopping Walker now. He went away, tearing up the track after the bell to cover it in 56.4 seconds, with the last 120 yards consuming just 15.1 seconds on the stopwatch. As he burst through the tape, far ahead of the second man, Ken Hall of Australia, with another Australian, Graham Crouch third, Walker felt certain that he must have passed the world record. Indeed he had. In fact he had run the mile in 3min 49.4 seconds, the first man ever to break the 3min 50sec barrier. A further measure of Walker's performance, indeed, of the steady erosion of the record, was that his time was exactly ten seconds faster than that of Bannister twenty-one years before. On that cold, blustery evening in 1954, a time inside 3min 50sec was unthinkable, all except to Bannister perhaps, who told reporters that the human spirit would conquer more barriers.

Walker's performance in lowering the mile record still further was one of the most perfect displays of running ever witnessed in the history of athletics. For days before the race the New Zealander had sat and pondered just how to tackle the world record attempt. Two days before the race he had run a couple of 200s in 22.9 seconds and, as he told reporters, 'I usually can't break 23 seconds for that distance so I felt as ready as I would ever be.' Walker also confessed that he had been worried about pushing himself too hard. The lap times had come up exactly how he wanted them and even this modest Kiwi had to admit: 'I feel I couldn't have run a more perfect race.'

*The New Zealander, John Walker*

# HIGH ALTITUDE OLYMPICS

Modern Olympic Games have become beset with problems far removed from sport. Politics, even murder, have dominated successive Olympiads and the names of Moscow, Montreal and Munich are all remembered as much for the off-the-field happenings as they are for the great sporting deeds which were enacted in the Olympic arena. It can be said that this interference began with the 1936 Olympiad in Berlin where the swastika flew alongside the Olympic flag. For some time after that, however, in London, Helsinki, Melbourne, Rome and even Tokyo, the Olympic ideal triumphed and the Games captured the headlines only on the sporting pages of the world's newspapers. But in 1968, when the Olympic Games were held in Mexico City, politics, riots, even sex, dominated the scene; and so it has been ever since. Those Mexico Games can be said to have heralded the arrival of international politics and intrigue into the Olympics, apparently for good. Yet, as always, there was so much happening in the arena, too. The Mexico Olympic Games of 1968 produced, for a variety of reasons, some of the most classic of all Olympic performances.

When it was decided to hold the Olympic Games in Mexico — the decision was taken at the 1963 meeting of the International Olympic Committee in Baden-Baden, there was no real objection to the IOC's apparently enlightened decision to take the Games to Latin-America, albeit to one of the more developed countries on that side of the world. The fact that Mexico City is 7,347 feet above sea level did not raise any comment at the time. But one year later, the Swedish coach of the great Abebe Bikila, Onni Niskanen, told the world of the 1969 Olympic Games: 'There are those who will take part and will die in Mexico.' His point was startlingly simple. The air in Mexico City is so rarefied that it takes a man used to living at around sea level more than one month to become acclimatised. In the Olympic Games there would be many men — and women — who would be attempting lung-bursting performances in search of gold medals. Niskanen certainly had a point.

The IOC had a rule which forbade any athlete to train at high altitude for more than four weeks in the three months leading up to the Games. Yet this put many of them at a serious disadvantage, for the Mexicans themselves, together with people like the Ethiopians and the Kenyans, already lived in high-altitude conditions. The French — in the Pyrenees — and the Americans — in Nevada — built special high-altitude training centres, but the fact remained that the problem was a big one and threatened to cast a shadow over the Games. There were other problems too, not least the political situation in Eastern Europe where, two months before the Olympic Games were due to start, Warsaw Pact tanks rolled into Czechoslovakia to supress the so-called 'Prague Spring' of the liberal Dubcek regime. Then there were the sex tests on female athletes. They were used in the Commonwealth Games, the Asian Games and the 1966 European Championships with somewhat embarrassing results for some competitors, though one of the happier aspects of these Olympics was that there were no incidents arising from the tests in Mexico. The IOC was also concerned with commercialism and two West German sports shoe companies were deeply involved. Then there were the domestic problems of the host nation. Riots broke out before the Games opened and for a time there was grave doubt as to whether they would take place at all. Eventually, order was restored and the opening ceremony took place — but against a backcloth of controversy. There was even the presence of troops around the new Olympic Stadium as Enriqueta Bailio, the first woman to do so, lit the Olympic flame.

But what of the Games themselves? It was a fact that the high-altitude had its effect from the very first day. Traditionally the 10,000 metres final — in fact there are no heats — was run on the first day and the winning time was 1min 48sec slower than Ron Clarke's world record. Poor Clarke was himself to finish sixth and in the most awful discomfort which saw him given oxygen by the Australian team doctor. The same thing happened in the 5,000 metres and the steeplechase. The first four past the post in the former event — Gammoudi, Keino, Temu and Martinex — were all from high-altitude conditions, and so were the first two in the latter — Amos Biwott and Benjamin Kogo. The final of that race was a strange affair. Biwott was a bizarre character so far as his racing went. He appeared to dislike getting his feet wet and his hurdling was 'rustic' to say the least. With a lap to go he was thirty yards behind the leaders. Then he suddenly upped a gear and screamed past them all to take the gold medal. There were many such moments in Mexico in 1968. But the men who we shall concentrate on in our search for classic moments are a long jumper from the United States, a high jumper, also from the United States, a Kenyan 1,500 metres runner, and a 400 metres hurdler from Britain.

Bob Beamon came to the Mexico Olympics looking for a gold medal in the long jump. He left the arena labelled as the man who had just jumped into the next century. Not many world records last for more than a few months as athletes are forever striving to beat the mark. Indeed, since World War II, only three world records in the Olympic events had remained unchallenged for more than a decade — Peter Snell's 1min 44.3sec for the 800 metres, Martin Lauer's 13.2 seconds for the 110 metres hurdles, and Iolanda Balas's 1.91 metres for the high jump — and after all, records are made to be broken, peaks are there to conquer. It is doubtful, however, if Bob Beamon's long jump record set in Mexico will be bettered this century.

A black New Yorker, Beamon went to the Games with a best mark of 8.33 metres. His

Bob Beamon leaps into the next century with his world-shattering jump in Mexico.

incredible talent for this event had never been questioned, but the man himself was not the most reliable of jumpers and on many occasions he had seen the red flag, not the white, hoisted to signal yet another 'no jump'. His two main rivals in 1968 were the previous two Olympic champions, Ralph Boston, a fellow American, who took the title in 1960, and Britain's Lynn Davies, whose 1964 exploits are recorded elsewhere in this book.

Boston was born in Laurel, Mississippi, in 1939 and was a highly talented all-round athlete. He reached world class in 1959 and in 1969 broke Jesse Owens's 25-year-old world record set in May 1935. Owens's mark was 8.13 metres; Boston took that to 8.21 metres and then proceeded to notch up 8.24,

8.28, 8.31 (to share the record after Ter-Ovanesyan had wrested it from him), 8.34 and 8.35 metres (which Ter-Ovanesyan had equalled in 1967, two years after Boston's latest record-breaking performance). The Russian was his main rival throughout these years, though Davies took his Olympic championship away from him. These were the men who, with Beamon, went in search of gold. In the qualifying competition both Boston and Beamon broke the Olympic record, while Davies repeated his 1964 performance by qualifying for the final with his last jump. Boston was the crowd's favourite and when his jump was recorded on the electric scoreboard they applauded him enthusiastically. Boston, however, showed no emotion. This was his third Olympic Games and he was intent only on regaining that championship.

Then came the final which proved to be both a sensational occasion and also a complete anti-climax. The sensation came with the first 'legal' jump of the tournament; the anti-climax when it was realised that the gold medal was already won, the other jumpers now simply going through the motions. Bob Beamon, at 6ft 3in tall and weighing 11st 10lb, was a skinny, lanky man, came up to the start of his run-up after the first three competitors had fouled. He bounded down the approach, hit the board to perfection and then leapt through the air, that thin air of Mexico City, until he had passed the point at which the sighting device ended its watch. Beamon fell into the damp sand amid a gasp of astonishment from those present. Out came the tape and someone whispered that it must be all of twenty-eight feet. Remember that the record shared by Ter-Ovanesyan and Boston was 8.35 metres and the twenty-eight-feet barrier was 8.53 metres, which had until that moment been considered unattainable. But Bob Beamon, twenty-year-old New Yorker, had missed out the twenty-eight feet mark altogether. When the measurement was announced it brought total silence while the significance of it sank in, and then roars of approval. The jump was 8.90 metres — an

incredible 29ft 2.5in. The Olympic gold medal was already won, Beamon had leapt into the twenty-first century.

It was the most astonishing single performance in the history of track and field athletics, indeed, in all sport. It was the biggest shock of any Olympic Games. Yet there were people who, even then, were ready to cry down Beamon's superhuman effort. They claimed it was achieved in the extraordinary conditions of Mexico's thin air, that it was achieved by a man who possessed little real technical ability, simply a natural ability, albeit a great deal of that priceless commodity. The purists were, of course, absolutely correct. But the man in the street had a simple questioning logic. He had heard them say that Beamon would jump right out of the pit — and he almost had. So why knock the man? At the end of the day his phenomenal record was — and still is — there for all to see. As for the rest of his career, Beamon never bettered 8.20 metres after Mexico and in 1973 he turned professional. It is quite likely, though, that his name will still be on the record books next century.

Until the 1968 Olympics, no one outside the United States had heard the name of Dick Fosbury, a 21-year-old student from Portland, Oregon. When the Games were over, Fosbury was a champion, perhaps the most

*Dick Fosbury's 'flop' revolutionised high jumping.*

popular champion of those Olympics, and, more than that even, he had given his name to a new style of high jumping, a style which the rest of the world has followed with great success ever since.

At the age of sixteen, Dick Fosbury was a promising schoolboy high jumper who was frustrated with his results using the unsophisticated scissors style of jumping. Fosbury decided to work hard on a style which would take him to greater heights. He spurned the traditional straddle — where the athlete drapes himself face down over the bar — and instead invented what has become known throughout the world as the 'Fosbury Flop'. It was a decision which was to change the history of high jumping. Fosbury reasoned that he could get higher by lowering the centre of gravity. He devised a technique of running at full stretch to the bar, then turning his back on it, and going over head first and backwards, thus 'flopping' over. It was a technique which earned him immediate success. He straightaway took his best jump from 1.62 metres before his change in style, to 1.78 metres afterwards. Two years later, and at high school, he had passed the two-metres mark, and in the January of Olympic year he jumped, indoors, seven feet for the first time. He won the Olympic trials in the United States with 2.21 metres and was now ready to unleash his new style on the world.

All the other finalists, twelve of them, employed the straddle style, and one by one they gradually dropped out. Dick Fosbury went on until, with his final attempt, he cleared 2.24 metres (7ft 4.25in) to take the gold with a new Olympic record. Fosbury had taken the imagination of the world and now everyone wanted to try his style. The 1972 Olympic women's champion, Ulrike Mayfarth, was a 'flopper' and so too was the 1974 men's champion, Jacek Wszola. Mary Peters turned to 'flopping' and improved her high jump so much that it was the biggest single factor in her pentathlon gold success. The sport owes much to Dick Fosbury. Not very often does one man change the course of sporting history.

There is no doubt that the runners of Ethiopia and Kenya have, for many years, captured the imagination of athletic followers the world over. In 1968 another of these great Africans, Kip Keino, continued in the tradition by routing the great Jim Ryun of the United States to win a memorable 1,500 metres. Kipchoge Keino was born in Kipsamo in January 1940 and as a sixteen-year-old was fascinated by the deeds of Kenya's first great runner of international standing, Nyandika Maiyoro, who came seventh in the 1956 Olympic Games 5,000 metres in Melbourne. Strangely though, Keino did not take up athletics seriously until his twenty-second year. Then he began with a three-mile race in 14min 17sec and was soon acclaimed as the Kenyan and East African champion. In the 1962 Commonwealth Games in Perth, Western Australia, Keino finished eleventh in the three-miles (in 13min 50sec) and set a new national record for the mile with 4min 7sec. On to the Tokyo Olympics in 1964 and Keino finished fifth in the 5,000 metres, only twelve or so yards behind the gold medallist, Bob Schul of the United States.

Up until that point Keino had only promised to deliver the goods. The following year he fulfilled that promise with some electrifying performances on European tracks. He beat Ron Clarke in two out of three 5,000 metres races, set a new world record for the 3,000 metres with a time of 7min 39.6sec, and came very near to the world record for the mile with 3min 54.2sec. Indeed, 1965 was a very good year for Kip Keino. He also won the 1,500 metres and 5,000 metres in the first African Games held in Brazzaville, Congo, and then went to New Zealand where he took Clarke's 5,000 metres world record, albeit only temporarily, with 13min 24.2sec. The feats continued into 1966. In the Commonwealth Games in Jamaica he completed a tremendous double in the three miles (12min 57.4sec) and the mile (3min 53.4sec). Keino's exquisite, loping gait was loved by the crowds and in the years after the 1968 Olympics he gained a gold in the 1972 Olympics steeplechase and the 1970 Commonwealth 1,500 metres and continued to parade his talents at everything from 800 metres to 10,000 metres. But it was in Mexico that he achieved his most classic feat.

Keino had already run in both the 5,000 metres and 10,000 metres, winning a silver in the 5,000 metres after a desperate finish in which Gammoudi just beat the Kenyan to the line. The 1,500 metres was one of the most eagerly awaited events of the Games. The front-running tactics of Keino and the renowned finishing burst of Ryun, the world record-holder, were expected to produce a memorable final. Ryun had enjoyed an amazing and swift rise to fame. His very first mile, at the age of fifteen in 1962, took him 5min 38sec; less than two years later he had broken four minutes and continued to clip seconds off that time. He went to Mexico as holder of both the mile record (3min 51.1sec) and the 1,500 metres (3min 33.1sec). In Mexico, and despite having suffered from glandular fever earlier that year, Jim Ryun felt confident of the gold medal, as well he should. But, the American reckoned without the form of Keino. Even though he had run in two gruelling finals, the Kenyan was at his best.

Keino's fellow countryman, the schoolboy Ben Jipcho, went away at a cracking pace, obviously intending to sacrifice any personal glory in a bid to help his illustrious teammate. Jipcho passed the first 400 metres in 56.0 seconds with Harold Norpoth of West Germany, and Keino, relaxed in his wake. Back in ninth position Jim Ryun was trying hard to stay in contention. Keino then took over and the 800 metres was reached in a fast 1min 55.3sec, Keino now strode gloriously away and 1,200 metres came up in 2min 53.4sec. Keino was so far ahead, and two West Germans, and Britain's John Whetton looked to be the only runners contesting silver and bronze. But Ryun was coming up hard with one of his famous bursts. He came past Whetton and Norpoth and as they came up to the final turn the American closed on Tümmler's shoulder. But the West German was having none of it and he forced Ryun

into the second lane for much of that bend. The effort required for this was too much for the American and although he passed Tümmler at last, he seemed resigned to the fact that he would get, at best, the silver. Meanwhile, Keino had won the gold for which he had been searching throughout these Games. He finished twenty metres ahead in 3min 34.9sec — the second-fastest 1,500 metres of all time.

It was the triumph of a high-altitude runner over a sea-level runner and yet even though Keino was used to such conditions, this was still an incredible time. The Kenyan said afterwards: 'I didn't have a plan to beat Jim Ryun, but we knew that he had a very fast kick in the last quarter and so I tried to run just as fast as I could over the first three laps. I'd had stomach troubles and when I get them, it's the end. That is why I had to run very fast at the start. I could feel the problem coming on over the last 200 metres, but I knew that I must finish.' And finish he did. David Hemery was the great British hero of the 1968 Olympic Games athletics competition. True, there was Sheila Sherwood, wife of the 400 metres hurdles bronze medallist, who took the silver in the women's long jump; there was nineteen-year-old Lillian Board, Britain's great favourite for the 400 metres who was caught on the line by the largely unknown French girl, Colette Besson, but who set a national record in taking the silver; and there were other Britons who did not win medals but who put up commendable performances. Hemery, though, was the national hero, winning the 400 metres hurdles in world record time with one of the most staggering performances of a staggering Games.

Hemery was born in Gloucestershire in July 1944 and he was a unique product of both British and American athletics. The family moved to the United States when Hemery was twelve years old and after graduating from high school in Massachusetts, he returned to Britain in 1962 and began his illustrious career. In 1963, Hemery won the AAA junior 120 yards hurdles title and also made his debut in the 440 yards

*David Hemery on his way to a world record time in the 400 metres hurdles.*

hurdles, running the race in 58.6 seconds in finishing third at the Midland Championships. The following year, Hemery entered Boston University and in 1966 he broke European indoors records in the 600 yards (1min 9.8sec), and 60 yards hurdles (7.1 seconds). In the 1966 Commonwealth Games, Hemery won the 120 yards hurdles gold medal in 14.1 seconds and then returned to Europe to equal the United Kingdom record of 13.9 seconds. In Olympic year, Hemery was coming up to full throttle. He began by equalling his best 440 yards hurdles time of 51.8 seconds and in his final American race he took the National Collegiate 400 metres hurdles in 49.8 seconds. He whittled that down to 49.6 seconds in Britain and was then

ready to face the challenge of the Olympic Games. David Hemery was the man on who the British contingent pinned their main hopes of a track gold medal. But no one could have foreseen just how emphatically he would take the Olympic title.

British interest in the heats was intense, for besides Hemery there were John Sherwood and the Tokyo silver medal winner, John Cooper. All three qualified — Hemery second in his heat, Sherwood and Cooper fourth in theirs. Hemery went off fast and after the first three flights was ahead of his main rival, the Italian Frinolli. But the Italian came back strongly on the final turn and it was here that Hemery appeared to falter. The Briton came back by the ninth flight to finish second in 50.3 seconds. He qualified comfortably, but it was worrying that, for a few seconds, his rhythm seemed to falter. Sherwood ran 50.2 seconds, Cooper 51.4 seconds, but the overall performance of the qualifiers was high. Six men got under fifty seconds and Ron Whitney of the United States was only two-tenth of a second outside the world record of 48.8 seconds set by his fellow American, Geoff Vanderstock. Rainer Schubert of West Germany lowered the European record to 49.1 seconds — one-tenth of a second better than the old one — when finishing behind Whitney.

The semi-finals found one British hope wanting. John Cooper, second in the 1964 final, finished seventh in his semi-final in 50.8 seconds, but that did not stop him being the first man to congratulate Sherwood who had qualified from the same race. Sherwood drew the seventh lane in this, the first semi-final. At the ninth hurdle he still held fifth place with the first four going through to the final. On the last flight, Sherwood rallied and got past Juan Dyrzka of Argentina, and Rainer Schubert of West Germany. Sherwood finished third in 49.3 seconds which took three-tenths of a second off Hemery's British record which he had set at the Crystal Palace. It seemed that Hemery would soon regain his record in the second semi-final. In fact, he finished in exactly the same time, behind Gerhard Hennige of West Germany, who set a new European record of 49.1 seconds, and the American Whitney. At the eighth hurdle Hemery appeared to change his stride pattern but still managed to qualify with room to spare.

All Hemery's thoughts were now concentrated on the final which the Americans,

*Showing their medals are British athletes David Hemery (left) who won the gold in the 400 metres hurdles, Sheila Sherwood, silver in the long jump, and her husband John Sherwood, the bronze in the 400 metres hurdles in Mexico.*

who had been prominent in the preliminary rounds, were expected to dominate, for the title had remained in the United States ever since 1936. But the Americans had also played host to David Hemery for a good part of his career and he had blossomed into a fine 400 metres hurdler. From the gun, the Briton went into the lead and he was over the first barrier marginally ahead of the next man. Hemery had obviously been saving himself for this moment. His speed was staggering and he launched himself into an all-out attack, a performance never before witnessed in this event. Hemery roared through the tape seven yards ahead of the field in an astonishing time of 48.1 seconds, clipping no less than seven-tenths of a second off the world record set by Vanderstock at the United States trials at Lake Tahoe. Second in 49 seconds was West Germany's Gerhard Hennige, with John Sherwood recording the same time to take the bronze medal for Britain.

The Mexico Olympics had its problems and its heroes, not least the great Al Oerter, who took his fourth Olympic discus title. Of course, there was Beamon, there was Keino, and there was Fosbury. But Hemery's performance was the most astonishing on the track and the United States coach Payton Jordan said afterwards, 'We always thought that David Hemery would be a threat in the 400 metres hurdles. He had competed in the United States and we knew his worth only too well. But I never dreamed he would run 48.1 seconds. That was possibly *the* performance of the Games. I just do not know where that extra half-second came from — 48.6 seconds, yes, but not 48.1.' David Hemery had achieved the ultimate and after Mexico he turned to the decathlon. He ran a new United Kingdom 110 metres hurdles record in 13.6 seconds, won a silver in the European Championships and in 1970 retained his Commonwealth title. In the 1972 Olympics, Hemery failed to retain his title at 400 metres hurdles, winning the bronze medal in 48.6 seconds, and then completed the set with a silver in the 4 x 400 metres relay. He turned professional in 1975, still glowing in the warmth of that performance in Mexico seven years earlier.

# ULSTER'S GOLDEN GIRL

When Mary Rand won the long jump gold medal in Tokyo, and followed it up with a silver in the pentathlon, there was another Mary competing in the event to find the best all-round track and field female athlete in the world. Mary Peters, born and raised in the Liverpool district of Halewood until she was twelve, but by now a firmly adopted daughter of Northern Ireland, had at one time been in third place in that 1964 pentathlon before slipping back to fourth place. Four years later in Mexico City, Mary Peters was back but, just like Tokyo, she failed in her two remaining events on the second day and finished an even more disappointing ninth. Most athletes who had been competing at the top level for twelve years, as Mary Peters had, would have seriously considered the wisdom of continuing on towards another Olympic Games. But Mary Peters, urged on by her coach and close friend 'Buster' McShane, had no thoughts of retiring. Instead she set her sights firmly on the 1970 Commonwealth Games in Edinburgh. That decision was the first step along a road which would bring her the ultimate glory of an Olympic gold medal at the third attempt.

The Commonwealth Games in the first year of the Seventies found the blonde girl from Ulster at her absolute best. On the first day she found the events which gave her a commanding lead; on the second she completed a fine performance to earn herself 5,148 points, then the third highest ever achieved under that scoring system. For good measure Mary Peters also became the Commonwealth shot putt champion, adding the gold to the silver medal which she had won in 1966 at Kingston. These were great fillips for the 1972 Olympic Games to be held

in Munich and before those Games, Mary left the riot-torn streets of Belfast for the sun of California. A Winston Churchill Fellowship enabled her to visit the United States and train under the best possible conditions, also taking the opportunity to renew her friendship with Mary Rand who had by this time married the Mexico City Olympic Games decathleon champion, Bill Toomey.

Mary Peters found the first day of her pentathlon challenge in direct contrast to the warmth of California. The West Germans had prepared a superb space-age stadium and surrounding complex to house the 1972 Olympics in the Bavarian city of Munich; but they had no control over the weather and as Mary and her fellow pentathletes came out for the first event — the 100 metres hurdles — they were met with a damp and cold day which threatened to chill the bones and stiffen the muscles. As Mary Peters looked up at the grey sky, she knew that this would be her last chance of an Olympic gold medal. At the age of thirty-three she was already the oldest of the Olympic hopefuls for this event; four years hence and she would be far too old to think about another attempt should this one fail. The 100 metres hurdles was a new event and it replaced the 80 metres hurdles which was run for the last time in Mexico City. In the first heat of the new race, West Germany's Heide Rosendahl therefore set a new Olympic record when she won in 13.3 seconds. The East German, Burglinde Pollak, finished second in that heat in 13.53 seconds and Mary Peters knew what she had to do when she went to the starting blocks. From the gun it was the tall East German girl, Christine Bodner, who streaked away to win in 13.25 seconds. Mary Peters was behind her in 13.29 seconds and when the times were adjusted, the two girls shared a new Olympic record.

After that first event Mary Peters found herself just six points behind the leader, Bodner, and seven points ahead of Rosendahl, the European champion, while Pollak, the world record-holder, trailed in fourth position. No one had passed the 1,000 points mark after the first leg of the pentathlon, but the girls knew that in the next event, the shot, they would need to amass around that total. Mary Peters's first putt measured only 15.03 metres (49ft 3.75in); and when Pollak reached 15.56 metres (51ft 0.75in) with her first throw, British hearts sank a little. But we need not have worried, for with her second throw, Mary Peters produced 16.20 metres (53ft 1.75in) which gave her 960 points. That was the winning throw and Mary now found herself forty-one points ahead of the world record-holder, and with the last event of the first day, the high jump, coming up. Mary Peters knew that this was where she must open up a big lead, for the following day presented her weakest events, the long jump — for which Rosendahl held the world record and the Olympic championship — and the 200 metres.

Mary Peters had worked so hard at her own high jumping, moving over to the 'flop' technique and nearing a height of six feet as a result. For Heide Rosendahl there were problems on that wet Saturday in Munich and she could jump no higher than 1.65 metres (5ft 5in), leaving the final battle to be fought out between Mary Peters and Burglinde Pollak. Mary struggled on her first two attempts at 1.71 metres (5ft 7.25in) before she presented herself to the bar once more and this time went over with an ease which made us wonder what all the fuss had been about on the first two desperate attempts. At the first attempt, Mary then cleared 1.74 metres (5ft 8.5in), but then kept the crowd waiting with baited breath at 1.76 metres (5ft 9.25in) before clearing it at the last attempt. There was something else happening in the stadium, however. Mary Peters, the blonde from the wretched war-torn province of Ulster, had become a great favourite with the crowd and even the Germans, so interested in the deeds of their own girls, found time to applaud her. Even the fact that the East German, Wolfgang Nordwig was at that moment taking the pole vault away from the Americans who had held the Olympic title since 1896 paled beside the lovable Mary Peters.

Mary's best in the high jump was 1.78 metres (5ft 10in) and when she cleared that at the first attempt, she knew that she could do it. No other woman could match her that day and suddenly Mary Peters found herself jumping alone, fighting a battle with no other competitor, just the bar. Up it went to 1.80 metres (5ft 10.75in) and again Mary cleared it at the first attempt. Now it went up again, this time to within half an inch of six feet — and yet again Mary sailed over at the first time of asking. Only at 1.84 metres (6ft 0.5in) did Mary Peters fail, and even then she all but cleared it at her second attempt. But what really mattered was the fact that she had taken 1,049 points from the high jump — and her overall tally of 2,969 points was a world-best at this stage of the women's pentathlon. Naturally, she was in the lead and went to bed wondering if she had done enough. Was her lead of 97 points over Pollak enough? With the long jump and the 200 metres to come, there was still no certain outcome, though Rosendahl, the world record-holder in the long jump, had slipped down to fifth place.

On the following day the sun came out and Mary Peters felt the warmth of it on her back and she thundered down the approach on her first attempt in the long jump. Alas, she fouled it and the red flag signalled 'no jump'. In contrast, Pollak jumped 5.96 metres (19ft 6.5in), and then Rosendahl, true to form, went so close to her own world record with 6.83 metres (22ft 5in). It was two inches better than the jump with which she had taken the gold medal in that event and earned her 1,082 points. Mary Peters then jumped cleanly for 5.90 metres (19ft 4.5in), Pollak went to 6.21 metres (20ft 4.5in), and then Rosendahl, now assured of first place, went all out to beat her world record but instead fouled the jump. Mary Peters now went for her last jump and cleared 5.97 metres (19ft 7.5in) to earn 902 points and keep herself clear in the lead with one event to go.

Mary Peters led with 3,871 points, Pollak was second on 3,824 and Rosendahl third with 3,750. The Ulster heroine knew that she stood no chance of winning the 200 metres,

*The strain shows on Mary Peters's face as she strives for pentathlon gold in the long jump.*

but she also knew that if she ran fast enough she would take that elusive gold medal. The last event was split into four heats with the leading seven girls all going into the final heat. Mary Peters, drawn in the third lane, went away fast, knowing that Rosendahl would almost certainly win but also knowing that if she kept in contention then she could clock a fast enough time to win the overall event. Sure enough, Heide Rosendahl hit the tape first, then came the two East Germans, Pollak and Bodner, then Mary Peters; the result hardly mattered, only the clock would now determine the winner. Rosendahl's time flashed up . . . 22.96 seconds. Then came Pollak . . . 23.93 seconds, then Bodner . . . 23.66 seconds. By this time the British camp had worked out that Mary Peters needed a time of 24.18 seconds to win the gold medal. The wait was only a few seconds but it seemed like an eternity for Mary Peters and her coach, 'Buster' McShane. Finally it was there . . . 24.08 seconds. Mary Peters leapt for joy — she was the new Olympic champion.

Her time in that last event had earned her 930 points and that gave her an overall total of 4,801 points — a new world record. Behind Mary Peters came Heide Rosendahl with 4,791 points, third came Burglinde Pollak with 4,768 points. If Mary was just ten points ahead — and if she had run her 200 metres just one-tenth of a second slower, then that margin would have been chipped away. The days which followed were a mixture of great happiness — when her father, who she had not seen for two years, appeared to tell her that he had flown from his new life in Australia to see her win her gold medal — and sadness when she received a death-threat from Belfast to remind her of the stark realities of what was going on back home.

But Mary Peters overcame that and other setbacks to take another gold medal, this time in the 1974 Commonwealth Games in Christchurch, New Zealand, in January 1974. The greatest setback of all was the death, as the result of a car accident, of her beloved coach, 'Buster' McShane. Since 1962, McShane had prepared Mary Peters for world competition and when that cruel blow came in the spring of 1973, the bottom all but fell out of her world. But Mary Peters is best-known for her courage and she summoned all her resolve, knowing that McShane would have wanted nothing more than to know that his star pupil was continuing to achieve what he always knew she was capable of winning. She went to New Zealand and won another gold medal — as much a tribute to 'Buster'

*Britain's Mary Peters seen here on the winners rostrum with Heide Rosendahl (West Germany) who came second and Burglinde Pollax (East Germany), third in the Pentathlon of the Olympic Games in Munich.*

McShane as to her own skill and courage. Then Mary Peters turned to face the problems of Northern Ireland. It would have been easy for her to have opted for some quiet life elsewhere. Instead she showed all the courage she had displayed on the track and began to work hard to improve sporting facilities in her homeland, including the building of an all-weather track in Belfast. Mary Peters proved herself to be more than just an Olympic champion, but we shall remember her best for those two days in Munich when she won the hearts of everyone who perhaps, even then, sensed they were in the company of a very special person.

# DAVE BEDFORD'S GREATEST DAY

One athlete more than any other was responsible for bringing back the big crowds to major athletics tournaments in London during the early 1970s. The flamboyant moustachioed Londoner, David Bedford, a great front-runner on the track — and no shrinking violet off it — assumed the role of a real 'character' in athletics, something which the sport had lacked for too long. Bedford was a kind of George Best of athletics, a performer of exceptional talent, and the kind of colourful personality who people will always pay good money to see in action. He was also a journalist's dream, someone to write about without having to employ the usual platitudes and clichés which so often dominate sports writing. At the Crystal Palace track in London, on an August evening in 1973, David Bedford did what he had been threatening to do for sometime. He shook off the disappointment of failure at Olympic and European level and ran the race of his life to bring a world record home to Britain. Dave Bedford, the runner who had promised so much but so often had struggled to deliver those promises, sat on top of the world.

David Bedford was born in London on 30 December 1949. On 19 April 1969 — aged nineteen — he broke his first national record when he ran 28min 24.4sec for the 10,000 metres. It was to be the first of many such performances. At one time Bedford held every United Kingdom record (except for two miles) from 2,000 metres to 10,000 metres inclusive, as well as the 3,000 metres steeplechase UK record. In 1971, Bedford took the international cross-country title, following in the great English tradition — the national team took the team title in this event from 1964-72 inclusive — and when he finished first out of 1,195 starters Dave Bedford won his first and only major international championship. Yet he kept breaking records — and these feats numbered among the top bracket in the world of long distance running. Bedford, however, could not produce his record-breaking form in the great championships of the world. In 1971 he finished sixth in the European Championships 10,000 metres; and a year later, in the Munich Olympics, he was again sixth. Bedford went into the Olympics after winning both the 5,000 metres and 10,000 metres in the AAA Championships — the former in the European record time of 13min 17.2sec — but fell away badly in the face of Virén's challenge.

Bedford returned from an Olympiad which had turned out to be a grave disappointment both for the runner and his many fans, and there followed a winter of discontent and a summer which saw him hampered by a hamstring injury and involved in a spot of controversy which saw him withdraw from the Maxol marathon. It was hardly the best preparation for him to defend his 5,000 and 10,000 metres AAA titles at the Crystal Palace in August of that year, 1973. His fitness was in question and he did not even rank in the list of British athletes who had run 10,000 metres inside 29min 35sec that season. He also had to contend with a class field at 10,000 metres, a field which included the Finnish runner, Seppo Tuominen, who was the seventh-fastest 10,000 metres runner in the world up to that point in 1973, having clocked 28min 18.6sec. To add to Bedford's already overflowing cup of handicaps, he went into the championships with only two races behind him that summer — a 3,000 metres at the FA Cup final at Wembley, and a two-mile race at Gateshead just two weeks previous to the AAA Championships. Bedford had been in tears after his Olympic and European failures and for some two months prior to the Crystal Palace event he had been under treatment for that troublesome muscle injury. Yet that in itself seemed to help the Londoner arrive at the Crystal Palace relatively untroubled by the press-

*Dave Bedford of Great Britain leads Burgos and Tasende of Spain in the 3,000 metres event at Cosford, which he eventually won in a time of 8min 0.8sec.*

ures which had surrounded almost all his earlier appearances. He came in just the right frame of mind, knowing that this time people did not expect a world-shattering performance, and yet that was just what everyone got.

He lined up for the 10,000 metres on 13 July 1973 with twenty-five laps ahead of him. From the gun David Bedford went into the lead and for almost every one of those twenty-five laps he led the field in one of the greatest displays of front-running that the sport has ever seen. Only for a short while, in the eleventh lap, did Bedford give way when Tony Simmons dared to hurry past the reigning champion. Simmons's temerity was

short-lived and by the time the lap was over Bedford had regained his rightful place at the head of the field and stormed away, this time yielding to no man. Bedford had covered the first 5,000 metres of this race in 13min 39.4sec — which would have been a world record for the distance prior to 1956 and up to the 1972 Olympics, would have been fast enough to win that race at the Games. Round and round Bedford went, his familiar red-stockinged feet eating up metre after metre of track.

Those poor runners who now found themselves being lapped, moved to one side to allow Bedford through, although Mike Tagg, Bedford's cross-country rival of old, tried his hardest to pace the Londoner for almost one lap. Inside the last two miles of the race, Bedford ran five successive laps in a time of 67 seconds and when he reached the bell and heard the announcer tell everyone that he now needed a lap of 65.2 seconds for the world record, he set off on the last 400 metres in search of the ultimate goal at this distance. The crowd cheered their favourite on and Bedford entered the back straight, gathered up his last reserves of energy, and then forged ahead for the tape. He crashed through it in 27min 30.8sec and thus became the first Briton to hold the world record at this distance. His second 5,000 metres had been run in 13min 51.6sec — which was the world record set in the Chataway-Kuts epic in 1954. Bedford's time clipped a remarkable 7.6 seconds off the record which had been set up by Lasse Virén when the Finnish policeman won this most classic of Olympic events in Munich the previous year — the race in which Bedford did so badly. Of course, Bedford's own British record, which he had set up at the AAA Championships in 1971, was also eclipsed; and so, too, was the Commonwealth record of 27min 39.4sec. Bedford was the fastest man in the world over 10,000 metres — and all this despite the perils and pitfalls which had beset him during the previous twelve months or more. There was little wonder that he told reporters afterwards: 'You know, tonight, everything just seemed to click. I've had only four weeks of what you could call real training. I would imagine that if I was fully fit, then I could take about one second a lap off tonight's time.'

On the following day, Bedford made an attempt to retain his AAA 5,000 metres title, but the effects of his world record run less than twenty-four hours earlier, coupled with the excitement and a relatively sleepless night, took their toll. Bedford may have worn the number one on his vest, but it was the Gateshead favourite Brendan Foster who took the title while Bedford finished fourth and looked to be in real discomfort. It did not matter, though and the previous evening's performance more than made up for the loss of his second title. Yet still Dave Bedford failed at the highest level in the search for gold medals. He went to Christchurch for the 1974 Commonwealth Games, feeling fitter than ever he could have done for his world-record. But he finished a disappointing fourth.

He thought that he might just have timed something around 27min 10sec, such was the measure of his confidence. Sadly, a leg injury which bothered him so much subsequently, wrecked any chances which he might have had of besting his own world record and taking his first gold medal in international track competition. Dave Bedford has often been the target of the press. When he trotted to a halt after that world record run at the Crystal Palace, he could not resist a glance towards the press box, a wave of his left hand, and a momentary V sign. The assembled gentlemen received and understood the message.

# KING BREN'S TYNESIDE EPIC

Saturday, 5 August 1974, was a special day in the life of Gateshead, that north-east town on the south bank of the River Tyne, a town so often overshadowed by its giant neighbour, Newcastle, sitting on the north bank. That afternoon, an athletics match took place to mark the opening of a first-class athletics track, the work of Gateshead Corporation. Running in that meeting was a man they call 'King Bren' up on Tyneside. Brendan Foster, born a few miles away at Hebburn in January 1948, was already a local hero. Almost single-handed he had inspired his home-town to become probably the most athletics-mad in Great Britain. He was already holder of a world record — 8min 13.8sec for the two miles which broke the great Lasse Virén's record in 1973. Now he was about to run an even more remarkable race.

Foster's very first international appearance, in the 1970 Commonwealth Games, had seen him take a medal when he won the 1,500 metres bronze with a time of 3min 40.6sec. In the European Championships the following year, he won another bronze at that distance (3min 39.2sec); and in the 1972 Olympics he finished fifth in 3min 39sec. It was the following year in which Brendan Foster established himself as a world-class runner. Beside's taking the two-miles record from the Finn, he ran a brilliant race in the European Cup Final, winning the 5,000 metres in 13min 54.8sec. In a strange race, Foster outfoxed all his rivals, and was doubly pleased to do so in the very first season in which he had seriously contested that distance. In 1974, at the Commonwealth Games once more, Foster collected two United Kingdom records. In the 5,000 metres he finished a close second to the Kenyan, Ben Jipcho, in 13min 14.6sec; and in the great 1,500 metres race involving Filbert Bayi and John Walker, Foster finished seventh and clocked 3min 37.6sec. At the AAA Championships in 1974, Foster won the 5,000 metres and for the first time we saw that mid-race lap of under 60 seconds. It was Foster's second successive AAA's 5,000 metres title and he lowered the time from 13min 23.8sec to 13min 27.4sec. Just after the halfway mark he ran a lap in 59.2 seconds. It was his new tactic to destroy the opposition — and it worked.

Three weeks later, Brendan Foster was back in Gateshead preparing for the 3,000 metres. His opponents for the race included Michael Baxter, David Black and Tony Simmons, the New Zealander, Dick Quax, and the American, Dick Buerkle. The British and Commonwealth records were both under threat, but an assault on the world record, held by the Belgian, Emiel Puttemans, was not considered to be highly likely. Foster had been short of track work and for him to beat the Belgian's record would require something really special. Foster's two miles record of 8min 13.8sec was worth approximately 7min 38sec for the 3,000 metres, which was four-tenths of a second slower than Putteman's time set in Denmark two years previously.

More than 10,000 people packed the stadium — easily the biggest British athletics crowd of the year — and this was a complete justification of the efforts of Foster and his fellow Gateshead Harriers, Max Coleby and John Crane, and other members of the local club. Perhaps it was the sight of all those faces which spurred Foster on to what was about to follow. From the bell, Mike Baxter set a tremendous pace — and kept it up for three laps. The lap times up to that point were: 60 seconds; 60.5 seconds; and 62.2 seconds until three laps had been covered in 3min 2.7sec. Then Foster assumed control. This was not so much a race between men as one between a single man and the hands of the clock. We can do no more than record the subsequent lap times: 61.3 seconds,

60 seconds, 62.6 seconds, and 60.4 seconds. The last two hundreds were 28.2 seconds and the last actual lap, 57.6 seconds. The overall time was thus 7min 35.2sec — the fastest-ever 3,000 metres. Comparisons are not always relevant but consider this. Brendan Foster ran in a time equal to two consecutive miles of 4min 5.1sec each (the conversion from 3,000 metres to two miles (3,000 metres is actually 1 mile 1,520.83 yards) was worth an 8min 10.2sec two-miles compared with Foster's world record over two miles of 8min 13.8sec). Foster, of course, went on to other great deeds before retirement in 1980. But none can have given him greater pleasure than his classic 3,000 metres before his own beloved Tyneside fans.

'King Bren' wins the 5,000 metres at the 1973 AAA Championships at Crystal Palace. A year later he sent his home crowd wild with a world-record run.

# ANOTHER FLYING FINN

Finland has had its great distance runners — the great Paavo Nurmi, Kolehmainen, Hockert, Ritola, Lehtinen and Salminen have all worn the blue vest of that country with great honour and dignity. In the 1970s, another great Finnish runner came to the fore and not only emulated his great predecessors, but actually went further than it was thought any athlete could reach. That he did so in two Olympic Games which were overshadowed by tragedy and political controversy did not take away anything from the individual performance of the man who was to be dubbed The Flying Finn of the Seventies.

Lasse Virén, a bearded Finnish policeman who was born in the little town of Myrskyla in 1949, came to the forefront of international distance running in the Olympic year of 1972, despite the fact that another of his countrymen, Juha Vaatainen, the European 5,000 and 10,000 metres champion was the man who everyone thought *would* be the new Flying Finn. Vaatainen won his titles in Helsinki and at that time Virén was just another runner, finishing seventeenth in the 10,000 metres and though improving in the 5,000 metres, still managing only seventh place. There was nothing to indicate that he, and not Vaatainen, would be the man to watch in Munich in 1972. But in that Olympic year, Virén suddenly jumped right into contention for medals at Munich. Prior to the Games he ran a 5,000 metres race in the second-fastest time of that year — just behind Britain's bearded hope, David Bedford — and then followed that with the year's fastest 10,000 metres. That was not all. In Stockholm, he then broke the world record for two miles, running the race in 8min 14sec. Now the sporting press began to

awaken to the 23-year-old Finn and the possibility that he might overtake Vaatainen, the man they all thought was a medal prospect. Indeed, when the Finnish team arrived in Munich, Juha Vaatainen was not with them. He had scratched from the 10,000 metres due to a knee injury, and had decided to arrive later and contest just the 5,000 metres.

The European champion was not the only runner missing when the heats of the 10,000 metres arrived. East Germany's Jurgen Haase, runner-up to Vaatainen in Helsinki, was also injured and missed the event. Yet on the last day of August 1972, the heats showed that even without the European numbers one and two, there was still plenty of high-class opposition. The first heat saw the Belgian, Emiel Puttemans, and David Bedford lap the 1968 champion, Kenya's Naftali Temu, and break the Olympic record in the process. Puttemans breasted the tape in 27min 53.4sec with Bedford just one-fifth of a second behind him. Virén took part in the second heat but showed no real hint of his own pedigree. The 1968 5,000 metres champion, Mohamed Gammoudi of Tunisia, won the heat and Virén was content to qualify in fourth place behind Mariano Haro of Spain, and the American Frank Shorter, one of the United States marathon hopes who was running in the city of his birth. The third heat produced an astonishing run by the big Haitian, Anilus Joseph, who burst into a fifty-metres lead by the time he went into the second lap — but who was lapped twice by the leaders who entered their twelfth circuit while poor Joseph was still struggling around his tenth! The man who passed the line first in this slowest of the heats was a sergeant in the Ethiopian Imperial Airforce, Miruts Yifter.

The 10,000 metres final found Yifter as the man who made the first break from the field. But the Ethiopian had no real chance of establishing a truly dominating position so early on and it was Bedford and Puttemans who gathered him back into the fold. For Bedford, thoughts turned to gold. The 22-year-old Briton went into this final as the great hope of his country, though the weeks immediately prior to this had been fraught with problems. Just one week before Munich, Bedford had been sensationally beaten in the 2-mile race in Stockholm and a stomach bug had sapped much of his strength. In addition he had the worry of allegations — subsequently dropped — that he had infringed his amateur status through advertising. However, along with Puttemans he had run that fast heat and now perhaps he could go all out for gold. At the halfway stage it was Bedford who led the field with a group of nine runners having separated themselves from the other six. Then disaster struck. Gammoudi stumbled and fell bringing down Virén with him.

If there is one thing that a runner fears most, it is to be sent crashing to the ground; yet within the twinkling of an eye Virén was on his feet once more and speeding after the leaders, though poor Gammoudi was badly winded and although he struggled gamely round for another couple of laps, he was forced to withdraw, his chances having evaporated with that tragic fall. Bedford still led, but the Briton knew that he did not possess a finishing sprint and, at the same time, could not find the power to draw away from the rest of the field, which he had to do if he wanted that gold. At just about 6,500 metres out, Virén moved up a gear and put Bedford to the test. The Briton was not up to it and as Virén quickened his challenge still further, Bedford fell away. Virén was now largely on his own. Puttemans, Yifter and Haro were still within reach, true, but the Flying Finn now looked a certain winner. At the bell, Haro had tried and failed to push in front. Now only Puttemans mounted a serious challenge. The Belgian was still there, the gap between them neither widening nor shortening, and both men were forced around the outside of a group of runners who were being lapped. With one backward glance, Virén killed any last lingering hopes that Puttemans might have had and found a new reserve of energy to take him to the gold medal in 27min 38.4sec — one second inside Ron Clarke's world record. Puttemans took

the silver in 27min 39.6sec; Yifter made it over the line for the bronze.

The 10,000 metres final had been an epic race between two fine distance runners, though once he had made up his mind to assume control, Virén looked unbeatable and always had the edge over his rival. Now we wanted to know if the Flying Finn could emulate Zatopek and Kuts and do the double of 10,000 and 5,000 metres. For the first time in the Olympic Games it was decided that there would be heats and semi-finals in the 5,000 metres, though as we shall see later, those semi-finals were never run. In the first heat, Bedford and Gammoudi qualified; in the second — the fastest — Puttemans clipped 7.8 seconds off Kuts's 1956 Olympic record; in the fourth, Vaatainen got home ahead of Britain's Ian Stewart; and in the fifth, Virén won with the second-slowest time of that round. That should have set the stage for the semi-finals, but tragedy struck.

On 5 September 1972, the Olympic Games had finally to accept that it could not opt out of the battle which politics was trying to inflict on international sport. It had to accept that in the most cruel and terrifying manner possible. In the early hours of that day, a squad of Palestinian terrorists, calling themselves Black September, somehow evaded the strict security which was supposed to surround these Games and got into the Israeli team headquarters in the Olympic Village. During the battle which followed, two Israelis received fatal injuries and the remainder were held hostage while the Arabs demanded the release of 200 political prisoners. The gunmen could not have chosen a more public stage for their demands. Suddenly, the bullet had come to the Olympic Games; not the bullet used to shoot at targets, but the bullet used to spill blood. All sport was immediately stopped and the Olympic Games took second place to the tense hours of negotiations now going on between the West German security forces and the Palestinians. For hour after agonising hour, the world watched and waited. The future of the Olympic Games seemed in grave doubt, certainly of these immediate

Games. Now the Olympic arena seemed incongruous, almost indecent, against the background of death.

Shortly after ten o'clock that evening, three helicopters flew out of the village. We did not know it at the time but two of them contained gunmen and hostages; the third carried West German officials. They flew to the airbase at Fuerstenfeldbruck and it was here that the West German plan to free the hostages went horribly, bloodily, wrong. It was planned that a team of crack marksmen would pick off the Arabs as they crossed from the helicopters to the jet waiting to take them to a safe country. Only four of the eight gunmen went over to the jet. As they returned, the West Germans opened fire, killing three Palestinians. The fourth managed to make it back to the helicopter and for over an hour there was silence. The West Germans now made their preparations to storm the helicopter, but just after midnight the carnage was completed. The hostages were killed, some by bullets, others by a grenade tossed into the helicopter by a fleeing Palestinian. In all, eleven Israelis had died, together with a West German police officer and five Arabs. On the Wednesday morning a memorial service was held in the Olympic stadium. The 5,000 metres semi-finals were cancelled, and the name of Munich was once more synonymous with tragic events. We had Chamberlain and his piece of paper, the death of the Manchester United footballers — and now this ultimate shame.

It was against this tragic backcloth that the 5,000 metres finalists lined up for their race. They were without Yifter, who had turned up too late for his qualifying heat and been disqualified. It was a cat-and-mouse start with no one prepared to take the initiative now that Yifter, a normally fast starter, was not there to set the pace. For the first 3,000 metres it was first the Briton, Ian McCafferty, and then the Russian, Sviridov, who eased the leaders gently round. This was now quite obviously a race more concerned with tactics than world records. Then the American, Steve Prefontaine, took up the challenge and four runners, Virén, Stewart, Gammoudi and Puttemans went with him. At the bell it was Virén who came through most strongly. Gammoudi lost touch with the Finn after a game effort to stay with him, the American could not find the strength he needed and now found Stewart coming up on him; but out in front there was Virén, running smoothly towards a golden double and a new Olympic record of 13min 26.4sec. Gammoudi recovered to take the silver, and Stewart had the bronze for Great Britain. The unhappy Bedford finished in twelfth place; Vaatainen in thirteenth. That same day, Finland's cup was full when Pekka Vasala shook off the challenges of Keino, Rod Dixon of New Zealand and Britain's Brendan Foster, to win the 1,500 metres with a kick from the last bend to make it a great day for the Finns.

Between Munich and Montreal, Lasse Virén added the world 5,000 metres record to his 10,000 metres record, though Puttemans soon bettered that; and the following year, David Bedford took the 10,000 metres world record from the Finn. The 1974 European Championships in Rome were a disappointment for Virén who finished third in the 5,000 metres and seventh in the 10,000 metres. All this time there was the growing challenge from New Zealand where Dixon, the Dutch-born Dick Quax — christened Jacobus Leonardus Quax — and John Walker were all threatening to take Olympic medals in 10,000, 5,000 and 1,500 metres. Virén arrived in Montreal after training in Kenya and in Colombia and felt relaxed, despite his disappointing performances of late. He had trained hard, but without undue pressure; and if the world now expected his reign as double Olympic champion to be ended by the Kiwis, then that was all right by him.

The 1972 Games had been overshadowed by the massacre of the Israelis; the 1976 Olympiad, as well as being fraught with worries over whether the stadium would be ready in time, was also the victim of political

*Lasse Virén wins the 1972 Olympic 5,000 metres in Munich on the way to his great 'double double'.*

*Dave Bedford seen here heading Lasse Virén in the two miles event in Stockholm, Sweden 1972. Bedford eventually finished sixth.*

nearly a quarter of an hour behind the eventual winner, Lopes.

It was Lopes, the 29-year-old Lisbon bank clerk, who took up the lead in the 10,000 metres final. The 5,000-metre mark was reached in 14min 9sec and then the Portuguese quickened the pace. With ten laps left, Brendan Foster realised that his chance had come and gone. Smets made a determined bid to push Lopes, but could not find the resolve required and now only Virén, who had been waiting patiently, was a threat to the little man from Lisbon. There were four laps left and the procession remained unaltered, though Foster was battling courageously against recurring stomach cramps; then, at the bell, Virén made his move, going into the lead so comfortably that in the final 500 metres he could find the time to glance back constantly at Lopes. He crossed the line in 27min 40.4sec, outside his 1972 Olympic record, but only the second man in history to retain the 10,000 metres Olympic title. The first man had been Emil Zatopek in 1948 and 1952. Now Virén had to attempt something that was beyond the powers of even that great Czech — to retain the 5,000 metres title as well and so complete a unique golden double.

Brendan Foster set an Olympic record of 13min 20.3sec in the heats, but the 5,000 metres final was not going to produce a time to beat that; in Munich the race had been run through the head, not the heart, and had produced an encounter which was a fine example of how to run a tactical race, and so it was on this day in Montreal. For the Olympic record-holder, Foster, there was only one possible tactic to adopt and that was to start fast and attempt to establish a firm hold as soon as possible. It was a tactic which was superbly foiled by Lasse Virén. At the halfway stage, the Finn suddenly took the lead and, as the rest of the field prepared themselves to go with him, Virén slowed down again and made the rest bunch up behind. No one took up the running, Virén and the rest all ran within themselves, and so when Foster made what he wanted to be the break, the rest stayed with him and his

forces. First there was the Canadian decision to bar Taiwan from taking part; and then there was the boycott by African and other nations in protest over the inclusion of New Zealand after the Kiwis rugby union team toured South Africa. Sixteen African nations, together with Guyana and Iraq, made a last-minute exit from the Games, taking with them 441 athletes and robbing, amongst other events, some of the distance races of some of their glamour. Challengers to Virén who were in Montreal included the Dutchman, Jos Hermans, who had refused to continue in Munich after the deaths of the Israelis; Brendan Foster; Haro; Carlos Lopes of Portugal, then the international cross-country champion; and Belgium's Marc Smet. In the heats of the 10,000 metres a Haitian once again caught the eye by storming on and on from the start, eventually finishing chance was gone. Now the Finn allowed the West German, Klaus-Peter Hildenbrand, to assume the lead; then it was the turn of the Kiwi, Rod Dixon. Still Virén waited, still running comfortably, still looking every inch an Olympian. Inside four laps from the tape, the Finn went, taking Dixon, Quax and Hildenbrand with him. Round they went again, and again, until the last lap found Virén still in charge. In charge he stayed, breasting the tape three metres ahead of Quax, two seconds faster than his Munich time but outside Foster's record.

It had been another superb performance from the Flying Finn. Lasse Virén had really started the race after 4,000 metres of jockeying had gone before. Former Canadian star, Bruce Kidd, summed it up: 'This guy Virén — he just mesmerised the rest like a rattle-snake.' Hildenbrand squeezed Dixon out of the bronze medal, there was the conjecture over whether Virén had been subjected to the controversial, though entirely legal, process of having a pint of blood changed before the race, thus giving him extra haemoglobin, the oxygen-carrying blood pigment, and then the man who had made history by becoming the first man to do the double of 5,000 and 10,000 metres — and then repeat it — got ready for the marathon. Though it was his first marathon, Virén finished fifth and when he re-entered the stadium he was given a bigger welcome than the gold medallist, Waldemar Cierpinski. No one cared that he had not won this race — they cared only that they had seen a man who joined Paavo Nurmi and the rest in the ranks of great distance runners.

# JENNER AND MOSES TRIUMPH OVER 'BARBARISM'

The 1976 Olympic Games in Montreal will be remembered most of all for all the wrong reasons: the horrendous cost to its hosts, and the fact that so many nations used what should be a purely sporting occasion to foster their own political ends. Yet during this Twenty-first Olympiad there were many supreme performances, not least by two Americans from widely differing backgrounds. They triumphed over what Lord Killanin described, perhaps rather pompously, as the 'retreat into barbarism'.

After the 1972 Munich Olympics, when there was the murder of Israeli athletes, this Olympic Games was the most security-conscious in history. Monique Berlioux, executive director of the International Olympic Committee resented the fact that this Olympiad did absolutely nothing to further the grand ideals of the Olympic movement. She described the claustrophobic security net as a 'collar of iron' and said that the absence of freedom was to be deeply regretted. The word 'anarchy' was also used and it was true that this Olympic Games had drifted as far away from the dreams of the founding fathers as it was possible to get. Apart from the security, there was also the incredible cost of the Games. Montreal's mayor, Jean Drapeau, had said that the taxpayers would not have to find so much as one cent towards the cost. At the end of the day they paid out around one billion dollars. Amongst the casualties of civic spending were a long-overdue sewage treatment plant, a sub-way extension, and several major parks plans. Ironically, even the city's recreation services had to be cut back in order to pay for the Games which, at one time, looked to be in grave danger of being staged in a half-finished stadium. As it was there were plans which never got off the drawing board, and even when the Games finished the bills still came in. The Montreal Stadium cost over fifty thousand dollars a day to maintain and though it was meant to be used after the Games were over, it was largely underused. For the Canadian city the Olympic dream had turned into a nightmare.

As if all this were not bad enough, there was politics to consider. The Canadians' decision to bar Taiwan from competing as the Republic of China surely broke the Olympic charter; and the decision by the African nations to boycott the Games after New Zealand's rugby involvement with South Africa. They wanted the IOC to ban the Kiwis; the IOC refused and sixteen African nations, together with Iraq and Guyana, refused then to take part. All this even before the Games began left the rest of the world wondering whether it was all worth it. The Olympic Games was meant to be a celebration of sporting brotherhood, not a platform on which nations could air their political causes. Thank goodness, then, for the athletes. When the Games finally got underway, and we could settle down to watch the sportsmen and women of the world — or at least that part of it which had decided to participate — do what they knew best. For those two Americans, doing what they knew best resulted in world-shattering performances. Bruce Jenner and Ed Moses set the 1976 Olympic Games buzzing with their own brand of demonstration. Jenner came to bid for the title of the world's greatest all-round athlete; Moses to fight for the crown of the fastest man in the world over 400 metres hurdles. Both achieved their goal — both in the most devastating and spectacular fashion imaginable.

Ed Moses was born in Dayton, Ohio, in August 1955, which made him just one month short of his twenty-first birthday when he flew north with the rest of the United States Olympic team for these Games. Moses stood 6ft 1in tall and weighed 11st 6lb. It is unlikely that any athlete has leapt from total anonymity to the ultimate of

*Ed Moses (USA).*

Olympic gold medal *and* world record-holder so quickly. At high school, Moses had never broken 50 seconds for the flat quarter; and he had never been inside 15 seconds for the high hurdles. Yet, at the age of nineteen, he ran 45.5 seconds for 440 yards during a relay, and 14 seconds for 120 yards hurdles. That was enough for his coach at Morehouse State College in Atlanta to realise that the longer hurdles event was perhaps Moses's best chance of reaching the top. Soon, Moses was running a 440 yards hurdles race in 52 seconds.

The decision to go for the 400 metres hurdles was one which changed Moses's life and in 1976, during the build-up to the Montreal Games, he clipped his personal best time down until he set an American record shortly before the Olympics. In March of that year, Moses ran 50.1 seconds, in April, 49.8; in May, 48.8; and in June that United States record of 48.30. Seldom, if ever, can an athlete have been in such peak form for an Olympic Games. Moses had moved relentlessly towards the world record set by Uganda's John Akii-Bua in September 1972. Akii-Bua's time of 47.8 seconds bettered the 48.1 set by Britain's David Hemery in the 1968 Olympics. Now Moses's coach, the burly Rev Lloyd Jackson, a man who wore a crucifix over his tracksuit, felt that Edwin Moses could not only win the gold medal, but also get very near to the Ugandan's record. If he did, he would be the first man to win the Olympic 400 metres hurdles using a thirteen-stride pattern.

The British hope of a medal in this event should have lain with 28-year-old Alan Pascoe. Pascoe had an exceptional pedigree as a hurdler. In the 110 metres hurdles he won a gold in the 1969 European indoor championships, silver in the 1971 European, and bronze in the 1969 European championships. Pascoe then turned to the 400 metres hurdles and won four out of his five most important races — the 1974 Commonwealth and European golds, together with the 1973 and 1975 European Cup Finals. His form as a 400 metres runner also saw him as part of the British team which won a silver in the 1972

Olympics, gold in the 1974 European championships, and silver in the Commonwealth Games the same year. During the winter of 1975-6, Pascoe enjoyed his best training period ever and he looked for a time of around 47.5 seconds in Montreal. Then disaster struck. An injury ruined the summer for him and when the Olympic team was selected, Alan Pascoe was included more on the basis of past achievements than on current form. He went to Canada with nothing to lose and decided to give it his all.

The first heats of the 400 metres hurdles were run in four races with the first four in each heat going forward to the semi-finals. Pascoe found himself drawn with Ed Moses in the final heat. In the first heat Tzioritzis of Greece won in 50.42, to be followed by Cuba's Alfonso (50.76), France's Nallett (50.77) and Portugal's Carvalho (50.99). The second heat saw the United States' Wheeler first (50.32), West German Schmid second in 50.57, followed by Perrinello of France (50.78) and Stukalov of the Soviet Union (50.78). Heat three and the qualifiers were Shine of the United States (50.91), Gavrilenko of the Soviet Union (50.93), Hewelt of Poland (51.39), and Bratanov of Bulgaria (51.84). In the final heat Moses went through in the fastest time — the only man to break fifty seconds — with 49.95, but Britain could be proud of Alan Pascoe who finished second in 51.66, with Parris of Greece (51.91) and Ferrer (Puerto Rico) making up the sixteen semi finalists in 52.45.

There were now two semi-finals with the first four in each qualifying for the final. Again Pascoe found himself in the last of these, again alongside Ed Moses. The first semi-final saw Shine (49.90), Carvalho (49.97), Bratanov (50.11) and Wheeler (50.22) go through. In the second semi-final, Moses produced a great performance with a time fractionally inside his own American record. His 48.29 seconds gave him a clear lead over the second man, Gavrilenko, who clocked 49.73. Alfonso was third in 49.84, and a brave fourth and thus a qualifier was Alan Pascoe who also broke fifty seconds with 49.95, which was Moses's time when he

became the fastest man in the first round heats. Nallett was just behind in 50.08, so Pascoe had done probably better than anyone had expected of him after his dreadful summer of injury, and qualified for the Olympic final. But it was Ed Moses about whom everyone was talking. Here was a man, unheard of outside the United States until now, who was threatening Akii-Bua's world record. Since he began in this event Moses had moved in inexorable fashion towards this point. All that remained now was to see whether the favourite for the gold could double up with the world record.

To win an Olympic gold medal and, at the same time, break a world record is the ultimate ambition of any athlete and on 25 July 1976, two athletes managed that feat. The first was Alberto Juantorena, a 25-year-old graduate of economics who represented Cuba and took the 800 metres in 1min 43.5sec. The second was Edwin Moses, the twenty-year-old student from Atlanta who scorched home in the 400 metres hurdles final with an incredible time of 47.64 seconds. It was nearly two-tenths of a second faster than Akii-Bua's record; and his winning margin of over one second was the widest-ever in this event. Not only that, his thirteen-stride pattern between the ten 3ft 6in-high hurdles was against all the coaching manuals. Counting the heats, this was only the eighteenth hurdles race over this distance which Moses had run. Of his unique stride pattern, David Hemery, the 1968 champion and former world record-holder, said, 'What we saw today was impossible.'

The United States also took the silver medal — Shine finished 48.69 seconds — and the bronze went to Russia's Gavrilenko who finished third in 49.45. Poor Alan Pascoe finished last of the eight runners in 51.29, yet for the first six hurdles he was level with Moses. Only when they reached the seventh obstacle did all the weeks without serious training take their effect. Then, Pascoe's body parted company from what his mind wanted him to do. The rest of the field surged past him and he had apparent difficulty in clearing the last hurdle. He went over the

*Alberto Juantorena of Cuba who was the 400 and 800 metres Olympic Champion in 1976.*

line almost at walking pace and leaned heavily on his knees as Moses and Shine went on a lap of honour. He gasped to waiting officials: 'My mind was running like a gold medal winner — but my body couldn't do it. I died at the ninth hurdle.' Nevertheless all Britain could be proud of Alan Pascoe. As for Moses, his coach, Rev Lloyd Jackson, said, 'What worries me is that he's beginning to think in terms of a twelve-stride pattern.' Jackson, of course, had his tongue in his cheek. From the start of his hurdling career, Moses had found that his long legs adapted more easily to thirteen-strides. That day in Montreal they carried him to glory.

Moses and Juantorena had dominated that day. The Cuban, after all, had run only four 800 metres before the Games, and none before 1976. Yet this 6ft 3in tall man, who

dedicated his gold medal to Fidel Castro, created his own revolution. With his big, loping stride and high backlift he decided to add the 800 metres to his speciality, the 400 metres. The former event had always been won by an athlete from an English-speaking nation but Juantorena was undaunted. He went through the halfway stage in 50 seconds, and although he lost the lead momentarily, recovered for that world record. Could he now add the 400 metres gold to his 800 metres? Not since 1952 had a non-American won that event. His rather naive starting style left him trailing badly in the final, but he recovered and in the final won by a clear margin in the fastest-ever time recorded on a sea-level track — 44.26 seconds.

So, the Montreal Games already had their fair share of heroes. Towards the end of the athletics competition they found another in Bruce Jenner, the decathlete from Mount Kisco, New York, who attacked from the very start and took the gold medal *and* the world record. His second day was the most efficiently devastating in Olympic history and it came as no real surprise, for since 1974, Jenner had been the world's top-ranked decathlete, losing only one of his twelve competitions, and that only after failing to clear the pole vault. Jenner, unlike so many great decathletes, did not rely on one or two world-class performances. Instead, he had no weaknesses in any of the events and he went to Montreal to compete against probably the greatest decathleon field ever assembled. He faced his greatest rival in the Russian, Nikolay Avilov. Jenner was holder of the world record with 8,542 points on the manual timing system. Avilov was world record-holder with 8,454 points on electric timing, and as electric timing was used at Montreal, Avilov, 1972 Olympic champion, was accepted as the world record-holder. A largely unknown Briton was Daley Thompson, sent by the selectors, not in the hope of gaining a gold here, but to gain valuable experience competing in the world-class field. After the first event of the day, Thompson found himself in third place.

117

*Ed Moses of the USA (right) runs a lap of honour after winning the 400 metres final at the Montreal Olympics. With him is Micheal Shine also of the USA who won the silver.*

In that first event — the 100 metres — Thompson recorded a time of 10.79 seconds. He was behind two Germans, Kratschmer, who the Germans felt was a potential medal winner, and the former world junior record-holder, Stroot. Jenner ran 10.94 seconds to settle into eighth place; Avilov's 11.23 seconds left him in twentieth position. In the long jump, Jenner recovered with a leap of 23ft 8.25in — only one-quarter of an inch behind the performance which helped him to the 'world record' during the United States Olympic trials at his home town of Eugen, earlier that year. Avilov, meanwhile, bettered that and closed the gap, while Daley Thompson took 859 points and slipped to fourth. In the shot, Thompson, nineteen years old and ranked twenty-ninth in the Olympic entries, dropped down to ninth

overall, while Jenner's putt of 50ft 4.5in lifted him to second overall with 2,493 points. Kratschmer was still in the lead with 2,562 points but Bruce Jenner was ideally placed. The day closed with Kratschmer still leading — the 22-year-old German student of physical education had 4,333 points — with Avilov second (4,315), and Jenner, with his best day yet to come, third with 4,298 points.

The first event of the second day was the 110 metres hurdles and here Avilov won in 14.20 seconds to leapfrog into the lead with another 939 points. Jenner's 14.84 seconds gave him 866 points. But in the next event, the discus, Jenner knew that he had the edge. He won the event with 50.04 metres, but it was still below his best and he knew that the whole point of the decathlon was not so much to beat your opponent but to beat your own best performances. The javelin followed and then Jenner went into the eighth event, the pole vault, nine points behind the Russian champion. Jenner finished third with 4.80 metres — Avilov having gone out long before, and Kratschmer was now in overall second place. There followed the javelin and the 1,500 metres to decide who would be in the 1976 Olympic champion.

This long day had started for Jenner and company at nine o'clock that morning when Lasse Virén and the other competitors in that afternoon's 5,000 metres final were probably still tucked up in their beds in the Olympic village. Long after Virén had achieved his 'double double', the decathletes were still hard at their task. The final discipline was the 1,500 metres and it was here that Bruce Jenner proved conclusively — if further proof were indeed needed — just what an incredible all-round athlete he was in this, his last competition. Jenner had 88 points in hand and yet he still drove himself round the last lap in a time of 60.04 seconds, a burst down the back straight which left everyone else for dead. Bruce Jenner was the new Olympic champion — and he had done it with a new world record of 8,618 points — a stupendous 164 points better than Nikolay Avilov's Munich world record. No less than seven men finished with over 8,000 points to underline just what a magnificent decathlon this had been. Kratschmer took the silver with 8,411 points, and the bronze went to Avilov with 8,369 points. Bill Toomey, the 1968 Olympic champion, had said that morning that Jenner would win the gold by 'hundreds of points' adding, 'The only way he can lose this now is by falling down.' Jenner, of course, did not fall down, and along with Moses, Virén, Juantorena, and company had ensured that sporting genius had overcome the wrangles which had beset these Olympic Games.

# YIFTER THE SHIFTER'S OLYMPIC DOUBLE

There is no wonder that they call Miruts Yifter 'Yifter the Shifter'. In 1980, at the controversial Olympic Games held in Moscow, this little Ethiopian of indeterminate age — between thirty-five and forty was as near as anyone got to pinning down his years at these Games — carried on the great traditions of his country, started some twenty years earlier by the great Abebe Bikila. Yifter stood only 5ft 3in tall, was balding, and looked considerably more than even the forty years of the top bracket of his estimated age. Yet he set the athletics world alight with two electrifying runs to emulate the greats, Emil Zatopek, Vladimir Kuts and Lasse Virén, in doing the double of both 5,000 metres and 10,000 metres gold medals in the Olympics. He did so with the help of fellow Ethiopians, against the challange of the reigning Olympic champion, Virén, and provided us with one of the strangest, most illogical 10,000 metres races ever run when he took his first Moscow gold.

Britain's hopes in the 10,000 metres lay with Brendan Foster, the hero of the North-East who everyone hoped would end his fine career with an Olympic medal. Miruts Yifter also had to contend with a fine Finnish representation, for besides the champion, Finland also rested great hope on Kaalo Maaninka, and there were the Ethiopian's own countrymen, Mohammad Kedir and Tolossa Kotu. Yifter, of course, had not competed in 1976 when his country joined the African boycott of the Montreal Olympics. Now in 1980, there were still boycotts — the most outstanding absentee being the United States after Russian involvement in Afghanistan. But the absence of the Americans did nothing to detract from the quality of the long distance events and with or without the Stars and Stripes this was surely going to be 'one hell of a race'. From the gun it was obvious that this assessment was going to prove accurate, though for reasons which were certainly not clear before the runners poured from the starting line and into the first lap of the Lenin Stadium where on the opening day, those parts of the world which chose to take television pictures from Moscow were inevitably treated to perhaps the most stunning opening ceremony in the history of the modern Olympics.

From the off, the three Ethiopians imposed their own strange style on the race. Throughout those first few laps they bewildered the rest of the field with a series of fast surges and then equally mystifying slow periods; they interchanged position constantly; and they completely outfoxed almost everyone as their challengers failed to work out their own individual pace. The Ethiopians tactics were now clear — they had worked out that by imposing these sudden changes of pace, they would surely burn off most of the opposition, and, sure enough, it worked. Brendan Foster stayed in contention until the middle of the race, and, indeed, the Gateshead man had led at the beginning, only to be set a series of problems to which he could not find the answer when Yifter and company began their cat-and-mouse game. The front group which broke away from the field comprised Yifter, Kedir, Kotu, the Briton Mike McLeod, three Finns, including Virén and Maaninka, and two runners from East Germany. With seven laps remaining, Foster was far behind while McLeod was also losing the battle to stay with the front runners. Two more laps saw the Ethiopians continue to vary the pace without warning, and exchange the leadership; now only the two leading Finns were in with a chance of catching the Africans. Then Lasse Virén, the great runner who had followed in the path of the legendary Paavo Nurmi, tried his kick but the Ethiopians held him back with remorseless efficiency. There was now no holding this strange little man from Ethiopia and Miruts Yifter took the gold. Virén had

*Miruts Yifter (Ethiopia) Olympic 5,000 and 10,000 metres champion in 1980.*

the winner. The Finnish champion had undoubtedly been troubled by the heat and humidity of the Moscow summer and the inevitable question was now posed as to whether he would have won in Montreal, had this insignificant looking little man from Ethiopia been allowed by his country to compete. There was no doubt that Yifter, though he might stand head and shoulders below most men, had become one of the giants of these Games.

Eyes now turned to the 5,000 metres and another question was posed: Could Yifter emulate Zatopek, Kuts and Virén in taking that race as well as the 10,000 metres? One factor which had to be taken into account was the fact that Virén would not be defending his title. The Flying Finn of the seventies had decided to save himself for the marathon. The first heats of the 5,000 metres were run on the day following the 10,000 metres and Miruts Yifter found himself in the same heat as the Commonwealth 1,500 metres champion, Nick Rose. Rose was one of three British hopes for this event — Barry Smith and David Moorcroft were the others and they all qualified for the semi-final, though Moorcroft was in considerable distress afterwards with the dreaded Moscow Bug. Rose was mindful of the Ethiopian tactics of the previous day, but in this heat. Yifter was simply content to sit in the pack until Rose decided to take the lead. The Briton looked strong — and so did the Russian Fedotkin. Then Kunze, the East German, came up to take the lead. That was enough for the Ethiopian. Though he knew he would now qualify with consumate ease, Yifter could not resist putting on a spurt to go through as the winner of the heat. Further classy running saw him to the final on 1 August where he made his attempt on the double gold standard.

During the interim period between the finals of the 10,000 metres and 5,000 metres, some considerable journalistic detection work had gone into discovering the age of this little chap who was, the battle between Coe and Ovett notwithstanding, becoming the great talking point of the Games. It was

burned himself out but Maaninka held on for the silver with a courageous sprint for the line to head off Kedir. Kotu took fourth place, while Virén, holder of four gold medals, struggled in fifth, some fifty metres behind

*Miruts Yifter immediately after taking the 10,000 metres gold in Moscow.*

still proving impossible to pin down his years, though the man himself thought that he might be thirty-seven, which was a two-year advance on the previous estimate. Whatever Yifter's age, it all added to the great mystique of the man. In the 10,000 metres, Yifter and company had worked out those astonishing tactics which had floored everyone. Now the 5,000 metres finalists viewed their race with great trepidation. What on earth had 'Yifter the Shifter' got in store for them this time? In fact, Miruts Yifter had, yet again, the unexpected in store in that he played his part with great orthodoxy — the double bluff, perhaps. For most of the race Yifter was content to stay in the pack and allow Fedotkin, of Russia, and his old rival Maaninka, of Finland, do the worrying from the front. The dimunitive Irishman, Eamonn Coghlan, also threatened at this stage.

It was time for someone to make the break and, as we all expected, it was Miruts Yifter who grasped the initiative with a moment of pure genius. There was one lap remaining and Yifter and his two countrymen were each well placed. Then Kotu and Kedir fell back and as the front runners approached the back straight it seemed that Yifter's own position was hopeless. Aleksander Fedotkin and Eamonn Coghlan appeared to have the little man trapped between them. Then Yifter stunned the crowd and his challengers. He caught sight of a gap on the inside and in the twinkling of an eye, he was through it and away. It was a move which took both Russian and Irishman by complete surprise and they had covered a further twelve vital metres before their minds registered on what to do next. The big, strong Tanzanian, Nyambui, was the man who finally went after Yifter and although he cut down the Ethiopian's lead by a small amount, he could not overtake him. Yifter passed the tape in 13min 21sec to take his second gold of the Games. Maaninka collected a bronze to go with the silver he had won in the 10,000 metres. The crowd went home to boast that they had seen 'Yifter the Shifter' complete a classic Olympic double.

# COE AND OVETT - OLYMPIC CONFRONTATION

On 25 March 1972, at Hillingdon, two youngsters were among the many who took part in the English Schoolboys Cross-Country Championships. Running in the intermediate section, one of the youngsters, sixteen-year-old Steve Ovett, representing Sussex, finished second behind Kirk Dumbleton of Hertfordshire. Ovett, then the current AAA Youth 400 metres champion, clocked 21min 42sec. In tenth place that day was fifteen-year-old Sebastian Coe, representing Yorkshire, in 22min 5sec. There were many youngsters listed that day, most of them to disappear into obscurity. But the names of Ovett and Coe, far from being lost in the wealth of lesser athletics statistics, were to become household names, not only in Britain, but the world over. Six years would pass before their paths crossed again — in the European Championships 800 metres in Prague on 31 August 1978 when Ovett set a new United Kingdom record with 1min 44.1sec, and Coe clocked 1min 44.8sec, though both were beaten by Olaf Beyer. Two years on from that day — eight years after that first meeting, Steve Ovett and Sebastian Coe met in direct confrontation for the third and fourth time. This time, though, their stage was the Olympic Games arena in Moscow, and their duel was about gold — gold medals at stake in the 800 metres and 1,500 metres. The most searching test of an athlete's skill and courage is at this level. We all waited to see how these two would fare.

These two great athletes have injected new life into their sport and since their Olympic battle of 1980 both men have gone on to greater feats, including world records at 800 metres, 1,000 metres, 1,500 metres and the mile. All of these latter feats are worthy

of inclusion in a book such as this — Coe's including 800 metres in 1min 41.73sec in Florence in June 1981, 1,000 metres in 2min 12.18sec in Oslo in July 1981, and a mile in 3min 47.33sec in Brussels in August 1981; Ovett's including the 1,500 metres in 3min 31.36sec in Koblenz in late August 1980. But the two Olympic races have been selected because of their special significance.

That does not mean that we should not be permitted to mention that incredible nine-day span in August 1981 when the world record for the mile changed hands no less than three times. First Coe ran 3min 48.53sec in Zurich to take the world record; then Ovett ran 3min 48.40 in Koblenz seven days later; and two days after that over 50,000 people packed the Heysel Stadium to see Coe win the IAAF Citizen Golden Mile in that astonishing time of 3min 47.33sec. That was an incredible race, eleven of the twelve runners broke 3min 59sec with Mike Boit of Kenya coming second in an African record time of 3min 49.45sec. The long-haired American Tom Byers acted as pacemaker that night and sacrificed any thoughts of a personal best to come in at 4min 21.6sec after setting a remarkable pace. During the third lap Coe was seen to stumble and it was later learned that he had caught Byers's heel, though no blame was laid at the door of the American who Coe later described as a helpmate 'out of this world'. The Kenyan Boit also contributed by pushing hard all the way to the tape, though he still finished some twelve yards behind Coe.

It was a race which capped an amazing spell; and just twelve months previously, in the heat of Moscow, Coe and Ovett had fought out another battle spread over a number of days. It was Coe's first Olympics, although Ovett had been there before, at Montreal in 1976 when he finished fifth in the 800 metres final in 1min 45.4sec and went out in the 1,500 metres semi-final. This was, of course, the Olympics which met with the disapproval of Margaret Thatcher and Ronald Reagan, amongst others, and Coe, Ovett and the rest of the British team went without the official blessing of the British

| | | 1500 M MAENNER | PROGR. S. 76 |
| | | ERGEBNIS | |

| | | | | |
|---|---|---|---|---|
| 1 | 405 | OVETT S. | EUR | 3:34.50 |
| 2 | 905 | WESSINGHA | GER | 3:36.00 |
| 3 | 505 | STRAUB J. | GDR | 3:37.50 |
| 4 | 105 | MORCELI A | AFR | 3:37.80 |
| 5 | 305 | ISHII T. | ASI | 3:38.20 |
| 6 | 205 | HILL D. | AME | 3:39.20 |
| 7 | 805 | SCOTT S. | USA | 3:44.00 |
| 8 | 605 | WALKER J. | OCE | AUFGEG. |

*The 1977 World Cup 1500 metres. Steve Ovett (405) won in 3min 34.5sec. Wessingha (905) finished second in a time of 3min 36sec.*

*Inset: The result of the 1977 World Cup Final 1,500 metres.*

Government. Both were ignored in the subsequent Honours List, though in the 1982 New Year's Honours they were both awarded the MBE, presumably for 'services rendered' post-Moscow.

The 800 metres event came first and with it the first confrontation between Ovett and Coe since 1978. Indeed, it seemed incredible that while these two names have been bracketed together for some years, this was only the third time that they had ever met. Sebastian Coe, with his world record of 1min 42.4sec from the previous year, was the great favourite for Britain's first gold medal in this event since Tommy Hampson in 1932 (up to then Britain had a great 800 metres tradition with gold medals in four consecutive Olympics from 1920). The champion, Alberto Juantorena, was missing; so too were runners of the calibre of Boit, Don Paige, Willi Wulbeck, and James Maina. Steve Ovett was, therefore, also a firm favourite to get among the medals — but it was to Coe that we looked for gold.

For the first time since 1924 Britain had three men in the final — Coe, Ovett and Dave Warren. Ovett won the first heat in 1min 49.4sec; Coe the fourth in 1min 48.5sec; and Warren came second in heat six in 1min 49.9sec. On to the semi-finals and Ovett again took the first (1min 46.6sec), Coe the third (1min 46.7sec), while Warren again finished second in his semi-final, the second of the three, in 1min 47.2sec. Now came the first of the two races for which we had all been waiting — Coe, the favourite, against Ovett in their first face-to-face match for two years. Over 100,000 people were in the stadium to see Agberto Guimaraes of Brazil break into the lead, followed by the Russian, Nikolai Kirov. Ovett was in a difficult position when the leaders bunched ahead of him on the back straight and the Brighton man shoved the tall East German Detlef Wagenknecht out of the way. The East German wobbled in front of France's Jose Marajo, but still Ovett could not see daylight. It was turning into a messy race with the Brazilian still leading into the turn with Coe sixth and Ovett seventh. About forty metres from the bell Ovett tried to get between Wagenknecht and the other East German, Andreas Busse, but they all but linked arms in a bid to prevent him from prising them apart. The bell was reached with Guimaraes leading in a funereal 54.55 seconds. Then came Warren and Wagenknecht with Ovett now moved up to sixth and Coe, the great favourite now running wide.

Soon after the bell David Warren took the Russian with him as he bid for the lead. Ovett followed them, but for some reason Coe decided to remain where he was, letting the leaders get further ahead. Now Kirov took over the lead and Warren dropped back.

*Steve Ovett takes Olympic gold in the 800 metres with Seb Coe unable to make ground after a tactical misjudgement.*

*Steve Ovett (centre) wins the gold, Sebastian Coe (left) the silver (both of Great Britain) and Nikolai Kirov of the Soviet Union, the bronze in the 800 metres final at the Moscow Olympics.*

With 200 metres left to run it was Kirov, Ovett, Guimaraes, Wagenknecht, and Coe and Marajo shoulder to shoulder in fifth position some ten metres behind the Russian. Into the finishing straight they went with Kirov still leading from Ovett. But Ovett was ready to strike and it was here that the result became inevitable. He drove off the last bend hard and went through to take the gold, running the final half-lap in under twenty-five seconds. Ovett's time was 1min 45.4sec — slow to be sure — and Coe was barely able to take the silver ahead of Kirov in 1min 45.9. Coe had, by his own later admission, run a terribly naive race. He had let the leaders get too far in front and when he did decide to go, the world record-holder found that he had left it far too late. His failure to respond at the critical time when Kirov broke on the second back straight was a fatal error. The race was untidy and a complete anti-climax to the great contest we had all expected. There was plenty of pushing and shoving and this was a long way short of the Olympic classic for which everyone had hoped. Still, there was always the 1,500 metres with Coe and Ovett the joint world record-holder. But would Sebastian Coe survive this terrible morale beating he had just suffered?

The heats and semi-finals went smoothly for both Coe and Ovett. Ovett won his heat in 3min 36.8sec, Coe finished second in his 3min 40.1sec, and the other Briton, Steve Cram, aged nineteen, finished fourth in his to go through. In the semi-finals Ovett and Cram ran in the first race with Ovett again winning, in 3min 43.1sec and Cram again fourth in 3min 43.6sec to become the youngest man in the final. Coe took the second semi-final in 3min 39.4sec and joined his fellow Britons. Even after the disappointment of the 800 metres final, this 1,500 metres still had all the makings of a classic. After all, did not Coe and Ovett share the world record of 3min 32.1sec? Had not Ovett succeeded Coe as holder of the mile world record? What was more, the two men had never met over either 1,500 metres or a mile.

The manner in which Sebastian Coe ran his semi-final suggested that he had rid himself of the disappointment which flooded over him after the 800 metres. He had been drawn against the East German, Jurgen Straub, one of his potential challengers for the gold medal itself, and the tall Russian, Vitaly Tishchenko, but though much slighter in build, Coe showed no hesitation in pushing his way out of a box. As he approached the last bend it seemed for a second or two that Coe had made the same mistake which cost him the 800 metres gold, but he accelerated superbly to finish in his second fastest time after the shared world record. Ovett, meanwhile, had run with all the streamlined assurance of which he is capable. The final looked like being one hell of a race.

There was no one from the host country in the final of the 1,500 metres, Tishchenko having been eliminated after finishing seventh in the semi-final. For Coe, that day in the Lenin Stadium was as much about pride as it was about medals. Everyone had thought that Coe would take the 800 metres gold, leaving Ovett to regard the 1,500 metres as the race he must win. But sporting fortunes have a habit of turning things on their head and the roles were reversed. Here was Ovett looking for the great double last achieved by Peter Snell, and Coe now running in what had become the race of his life. For the first 800 metres of this final the easy pace seemed tailor-made for the power of Ovett. At the end of the first 400 metres it was clear that this was going to be no world record-breaking race. Straub went through first in 61.6 seconds, then Coe (61.7 seconds), Cram (61.7 seconds), Marajo (61.8 seconds), Ovett (61.8 seconds), Andreas Busse of East Germany (61.9 seconds) and Vittorio Fontenella of Italy (61.9 seconds). Through the second 400 metres, Straub, the East German record-holder retained the lead with Coe behind him, followed by Ovett and Cram. The absence of Filbert Bayi had robbed the race of any real chance of lowering the record, but Coe must have been delighted that Straub had decided to grasp the initiative. During that second lap Ovett was content to drop in behind Straub and Coe, occasionally coming up to his great rival's shoulder. But when the East German began to stretch his lead, Coe found the luxury of space which he had been denied in the shorter final.

The second lap was even slower than the first — in 63.3 seconds — giving the time for the first half of the race as 2min 4.9sec. It was obvious now, as Straub, Coe and Ovett went through in that order, that this was now a three-man race. Now, with 700 metres left to run, the race began in earnest. Straub, realising that if the slow pace continued into the last lap, then he was dead in the face of Coe's and Ovett's blistering pace, decided at this point to head for home. Yet Straub's decision was just what Sebastian Coe wanted. As the East German sped away, so Coe went with him tucked behind him by about three metres. Ovett was just a stride behind in third place and any number of combinations were now possible at the finish. At the bell — 1,200 metres having been run — it was Straub (2min 59.1sec), Coe (2min 59.5sec) and Ovett (2min 59.7sec). Just as the pace had been so pedestrian in the first half of the race, so it was frantic now. Straub had covered the third 400 metres in 54.2 seconds, and the East German was going faster now. Along the back straight he went with Coe four metres behind, and Ovett two metres behind Coe. At the far reaches of the final bend Coe accelerated and with a devastating burst of speed came off ahead of Straub. Ovett was also putting in his effort, but into the straight Coe 'double-kicked' some eighty metres out. Ovett tried to stay in contention but he could not pass Straub. Coe, meanwhile, was winging his way to Olympic glory.

At the tape it was Sebastian Coe (3min 38.4sec), Straub (3min 38.8sec) and Ovett (3min 39sec). Overall, the times were quite ordinary and yet the second half of the race was quite extraordinary. Coe covered the last 400 metres in 52.2 seconds, the last 100 metres in 12.7 seconds. The last 700 metres had taken 1min 33.5sec — an 800 metres speed of 1min 46.9sec. Coe had, athletically speaking, come back from the dead with a tremendous display of physical strength and courage — and an equal amount of mental stamina. It had been a great race and perhaps the greatest moment of all was when Ovett congratulated Coe, for the press had so often wanted to believe that there was some 'vendetta' between the two. Nothing could have been further from the truth. Said Ovett: 'Seb was a worthy winner. I just couldn't lift myself after the 800 metres'.

That was true. Just as Coe had found himself unable to respond to Ovett's lead in the 800 metres, so Ovett had been unable to find his customary acceleration at that critical point. Yet he, too, had run a fine race and unlike the 800 metres — a race run like a novice event — the 1,500 metres had been a classic affair. Coe told reporters that his gold medal was for all the middle distance runners of Great Britain. Indeed, that country was fortunate to have two such fine runners in the same race in Moscow. The 800 metres was forgotten; the 1,500 metres had more than made up for it. Sebastian Coe and Steve Ovett, though both to be dogged by injury would go on to greater deeds, more world records, more classic races.

# MOORCROFT'S LATE RUN TO INSTANT GLORY

The music blares from the disco in a plush Oslo hotel and athletes, now relieved of the tension built up over the days spent preparing for their own particular event, can now let down their hair and relax for a while before picking up the more frugal life of their training routines once more. But even as they dance, or sit and just soak up the atmosphere, the talk is still of athletics and of one particular man who has, that very evening, stunned almost to silence a crowd in the tiny Bislett Stadium in Norway's capital with a run over 5,000 metres. It has left the headline writers feverishly preparing the following day's newspapers scratching their heads in search of a superlative which will fully justify the incredible performance which has been enacted some time earlier. Ironically, the man who has achieved this feat is not at the disco in the Panorama Sommerhotel. Instead he is out among the pine trees, drinking in the cool Norwegian summer night which is rapidly enveloping him. The midnight hour approaches and David Moorcroft, a 29-year-old former teacher from Coventry, the city in the heart of what was once the thriving British motor industry, is trying to come to terms with what he has just done. Moorcroft, until that day without even a British record to his name, has advanced the running of the 5,000 metres to such an extent that the inevitable comparisons with the greats — Nurmi, Zatopek, Kuts and Chataway — leaves those performers trailing in the blistering wake of this man who had fought injury and painful operations to burst from relative anonymity to world acclaim.

Yet those who follow athletics closely knew all about David Moorcroft, the man whose name was now a household word in Britain, long before his world-beating run in the Bislett Stadium on that July day in 1982. When he was the first male winner of the Kraft Scholarship in 1977 — being named in preference to Steve Ovett, incidentally — they knew that the honour could not have gone to a more personable and worthy athlete. A year earlier he had reached the final of the Olympic 1,500 metres and had shown a consistency which Ovett, eliminated at the semi-final stage, surely lacked at that stage of his career. Moorcroft came home from those Montreal Olympics and at the Crystal Palace he gained his first taste of real recognition when he took on the world 'metric mile' record-holder, Filbert Bayi, and beat him in the Emsley Carr Mile. Suddenly the name of David Moorcroft began to register with athletics promoters and offers came pouring in. Off Moorcroft went to New Zealand, but it was an unhappy time and he was forced to return home with a nagging back injury which was diagnosed as two impacted vertebrae. Twelve months of treatment followed, including a winter in New Zealand to escape the rigours of the cold British winter, and then Dave Moorcroft was ready for the Commonwealth Games and the European Championships. All the pain and hard work was now rewarded. A Commonwealth 1,500 metres gold medal was followed by a bronze in the European 1,500 metres.

But there were young men called Steve Ovett and Sebastian Coe also in the 1,500 metres and David Moorcroft knew that he did not possess enough speed over that distance to seriously compete with these young lions. With that he moved up to the 5,000 metres — and here came up against another problem, more serious in its effect. Moorcroft had always suffered from stiff legs after a 1,500 metres race; now he found that after a 5,000 metres race he was, to put it into his own words 'in absolute agony . . . it was murder . . . my calves were rock-hard.' Yet even while he was still running 1,500 metres, Moorcroft had never been one to neglect his long-distance running and in the

129

Olympic year of 1976, he had finished second in the 9-mile English Cross-Country Championships, so even then the miler had shown his undoubted talents for the longer races. In 1980, in the Moscow Olympics which were boycotted by the United States in protest over Russian tanks in Afghanistan, Moorcroft was one of the many British athletes who ignored the advice of the Thatcher Government and went to Moscow. It might have been a memorable 5,000 metres for David Moorcroft in that sweltering Russian summer, but the unseen hand which scripts great sporting moments had other ideas. He was afflicted by the infamous Moscow Bug and failed to get beyond the heats; and to compound the misery his coach John Anderson — they have been together since 1969 — also fell a victim and had to leave the Olympic arena in an ambulance.

In 1981 Moorcroft won the European Cup 5,000 metres and again showed that he was a truly fine athlete. Yet even though he told *Athletics Weekly* in a 1975 interview: 'There are obviously a lot of people able to reach the periphery of world class; some people are able to reach world class, and one or two become top of the pile, My aim is to become top of that pile . . . .' David Moorcroft still seemed to lack the ultimate spark which would make him into a world-beater. Of course, he had the problem of his legs, a problem not uncommon among top athletes including the great New Zealander John Walker, the first man to break 3min 50sec for the mile. It is a simple problem, but a devastating one for a runner. The muscle sinews constrict and are therefore unable to expand as they must when the athlete's blood is flowing fast. They lack the elasticity which is vital if the muscles are to expand properly. In September 1981, Moorcroft entered hospital to have the operation which would overcome the handicap which left him with chronically sore legs after each race. The surgeon opened Moorcroft's calves and slit the sheaths. With calf muscles now decompressed, David Moorcroft was now fully fit for almost the first time since he took up running.

In every way Moorcroft's life seemed settled. His relationship with coach Anderson was good; his marriage to Lynda, his childhood sweetheart was happy; their seven-year marriage had been blessed with a fine son — now fourteen months old; and now he had a stimulating job. Moorcroft had been trained as a teacher and did work in that profession for a time. But in the build-up the 1980 Olympics he tried, again in his own words, to become a 'full-time athlete because that's what I thought you had to do.' But David Moorcroft is the kind of man who needs to be active and he found that he was getting up later and that the hours around his two-hour daily training session were wasting away into boredom. So, after a good winter's training in New Zealand, he came back to his hometown and a job with youngsters in the Coventry and Warwickshire Award Trust. Originally, the idea was to promote the Duke of Edinburgh's Award Scheme and to work with Coventry City Football Club to give youngsters a chance to develop sporting talent. The work suited David Moorcroft well; he found the stimulus of helping the young unemployed of Coventry particularly rewarding.

So, all in the Moorcroft garden was apparently rosy when he went to Oslo in July 1982. His immediate aim was to beat Brendan Foster's eight-year-old British record of 13min 14.6sec. To that end, Moorcroft knew he would have to better considerably his own personal best of 13min 20.51sec, but he felt in great shape. His only nagging concern was just what tactics would be best for this race against a field which included Henry Rono, the Kenyan whose world record, set on this very same Bislett track in June 1978, stood at 13min 6.20 sec. Moorcroft went for a long walk through the pine trees to prepare his mind for the immediate task. He mused on the fact that he was fifty-seventh in the list of the best 5,000 metres runners; on the fact that, after his 5,000 metres European Cup win and on the day of the World Cup, he was on an operating table in St Gerard's Hospital, Birmingham, oblivious to the fact that a surgeon's knife was slicing delicately

David Moorcroft wins
the Bannister Mile at
the Crystal Palace, run
to celebrate the first
sub-four minute mile
twenty-five years
earlier in 1954.
Moorcroft shattered
the 5,000 metres world
record in 1982 with one
of the most astonishing
runs in the history of
athletics.

into his calves to perform the operation known as 'deep facia split'; and then Moorcroft glanced down at the five-inch scars which were still a reminder of that operation which had unlocked the key to this day.

Then he went back to the stadium 'nervous as a kitten' to make the final mental preparations.

The first 1,000 metres of this race was run almost at a dither. It was at that point that

131

David Moorcroft decided to go away on his own. So supremely confident of his own fitness, Moorcroft showed the rest of that field such a clean pair of heels that by the 2,000 metres stage he was on the record schedule; at 3,000 metres he had increased the pace still further to be ten seconds ahead of the schedule; and one kilometre after that he was twelve seconds in front. At the bell he knew that not only Foster's British record was in sight, but that he was also almost certain to take the world record if only nothing disastrous overtook him. Moorcroft, if indeed he was at all worried, need not have concerned himself. Though his strength was now naturally flagging, he still found the effort required to take him through the last 400 metres of this race in under fifty-nine seconds. Moorcroft hit the tape amid almost stunned silence, for this young man, fifty-seventh in the world at the start of the race, had clipped a staggering 5.78 seconds off the world record set by Rono and had come within a few fractions of the sensational thirteen-minute barrier.

One hundred and twenty yards behind Moorcroft came poor Henry Rono, the Kenyan who could only watch open-mouthed as his world record was shattered before his eyes. Even the second man in — American Ralph King — could only clock 13min 20.85sec compared to Moorcroft's new world record of 13min 0.42sec. The Bristolian, Nick Rose, clocked 13min 21.29sec — and Rono, now very emphatically the ex-world record-holder was 3.85 seconds behind Rose. For all but a couple of laps, Moorcroft had run without the benefit of a pace-maker, which made his performance all that more sensational, and for most of the time the race took on the appearance of a solitary time trial. The second man, Ralph King, was so far behind Moorcroft that he thought the Coventry man was a back-marker who was about to be lapped and that he, the American, was about to win the race. Consider also this: Chataway and Kuts fought what was described at the time as the greatest 5,000 metres battle ever, in 1954 — Moorcroft would have left them nearly a lap behind; Emil Zatopek, the triple Olympic gold medallist of 1952, would have been over a lap behind; and Paavo Nurmi, the Flying Finn and 'the greatest ever' would have trailed Moorcroft by almost one and a half minutes! Yes, whatever else he achieves in the world of distance running, David Moorcroft that evening became one of the sport's immortals.

Afterwards he told reporters: 'I don't usually lead but the Kenyans were running fast and slow over the first couple of laps that I knew I would never beat Brendan Foster's record. I was running well and feeling great, so I decided to go. I felt quite comfortable until about five laps to go. As I came up to the bell I knew that the world record was mine for the taking. I'm stunned, at fifty-seventh in the world it would have been supreme arrogance to suggest that I could beat the world record. I set out with the idea of passing Brendan's British record and after running my recent mile in 3min 49.34sec and some good road relays I felt I could do that. I always felt that I could do well at 5,000 metres but it's taken some time coming. Now it's magic!' The television audience round the world who saw Moorcroft's run no doubt agreed. Ten days later, at the Crystal Palace, Moorcroft was in action again. On 17 July he broke the 3,000 metres European record with 7min 32.79sec — the second-fastest 3,000 metres ever run and only 0.69 seconds off Rono's four-year-old world record. David Moorcroft was showing the world that his greatness was no one-night sensation.

# DALEY THOMPSON REGAINS HIS WORLD RECORD

In 1976, when the American Bruce Jenner was winning the gold medal in the Olympic decathlon — and breaking the world record at the same time — a nineteen-year-old Briton called Daley Thompson, of the Essex Beagles Club, was competing in his first Olympic Games. Thompson, as we have already seen, was sent, not to seriously challenge for gold, but to gain invaluable experience against the top decathletes in the world. The decision to send him was justified in the next Olympic Games, in Moscow in 1980, when Daley Thompson took the gold medal, albeit against a field which numbered the Americans, and the 1976 silver medallist and current world champion, among its absentees. A lot of things had happened to Thompson since that 1976 Olympics, when he was still a 'greenhorn', and 1980 when he won the gold. Earlier in that Moscow Olympic year, he had broken the world record with 8,622 points in the Austrian town of Gotzis; less than a month later, West Germany's Guido Kratschmer, the man who was runner-up to Jenner in Montreal, took it back from him with a score of 8,649 points at Filderstadt-Barnhausen. In May 1982, Daley Thompson went back to that Austrian town, scene of his first world record triumph, to attempt to wrest back that crown.

This was a different Thompson from the bumptious youngster who we had become used to seeing on our television screens. His wit and easy manner, coupled with a confidence which belied his age, made him a natural television personality; and when he was not testing himself in some artificial tests of skill which bore little or no relation to the real world of athletics, Thompson was appearing on this programme or that, bub-

bling over with an infectious enthusiasm, but which some of his fellow athletes found irritating, and, to loosely quote one of them, Daley Thompson was in danger of becoming a 'pain in the nether regions'. Yet all this hid the true dedication of the athlete. Thompson continued to train hard, compete regularly for the Essex Beagles in relatively minor meetings far removed from the glamour of the Olympic arena.

For the six months prior to his bid to recapture the world record, Thompson had been training, eight hours a day, in the sunshine of California. His ambitions were reported to be fairly uncomplicated — simply to take the world record beyond 9,000 points, to retain his Olympic title against the best in the world in Los Angles in 1984, and to become one of his sport's first millionaires. When he arrived in Gotzis in May 1982, Daley Thompson stood on the threshold of realising at least one of those ambitions, a supremely fit 23-year-old who looked quite capable of taking the world record into the 9,000 points mark.

It is interesting, at this stage, to recall the relative performances of Thompson and Kratschmer in taking their respective world records:

Daley Thompson (8,622 points at Gotzis on 17-18 May 1980) 100 metres, 10.55 seconds; long jump, 7.72 metres; shot, 14.46 metres; high jump, 2.11 metres; 400 metres, 48.04 seconds; (halfway score: 4,486 points); 110 metres hurdles, 14.37 seconds; discus, 42.98 metres; pole vault, 4.90 metres; javelin, 65.38 metres; 1,500 metres, 4min 25.5sec.

Guido Kratschmer (8,649 points at Filderstadt-Barnhausen on 13-14 June 1980) 100 metres, 10.58 seconds; long jump, 7.80 metres; shot, 15.47 metres; high jump 2.00 metres; 400 metres, 48.04 seconds; (halfway score: 4,480 points); 110 metres hurdles, 13.92 seconds; discus, 45.52 metres; pole vault, 4.60 metres; javelin, 66.50 metres; 1,500 metres, 4min 24.15sec.

*Daley Thompson (G.B.) decathlon gold medallist.*

The mild climate of Gotzis had made this spot a highly popular place for athletes trying to become the most versatile and talented athlete in the world over ten arduous disciplines. There is no doubt that this is the most searching — both mentally and physically — of all athletics competitions. Thompson was bidding to follow some of the greatest names in the sport.

Guido Kratschmer was not competing on this May weekend and Thompson was certain favourite to win the competition, his only serious rival being another West German, Jurgen Hingsen. But Thompson's real battle was with himself. It was his own best marks which he would have to attack. Thompson began the first day with confidence. In the first event, the 100 metres, he was only a fraction outside his personal best with 10.49 seconds. In the long jump he had a best of 7.95 metres (26ft 1in). In the shot, he consolidated still further with 15.31 metres (50ft 2.25in), and then leapt 2.08 metres (6ft 9.75in) in the high jump, to put himself 113 points ahead of Kratschmer's world record schedule. The last event of the day was the 400 metres and here Daley Thompson was in absolutely superb form. He recorded a personal best of 46.86 seconds to end the day with 4,632 points, easily the best ever recorded at that stage.

Thompson began the second day knowing that only the weather or an accident could bar his way from regaining his world record from Kratschmer. The day's first event was the 110 metres hurdles which he won in 14.31 seconds, attacking the race in his aggressive, though hardly classic style. The discus came next and this was his weakest discipline. But Daley Thompson had built up such a commanding score that he knew he had room for mistakes. He made none and his throw of 44.34 metres (145ft 5.5in) was better than his world record performance of two years earlier. The weather now deteriorated, but despite the rain, Thompson pole vaulted 4.90 metres (16ft 1in) and then threw the javelin 60.52 metres (198ft 6.5in). There remained only the 1,500 metres and Daley Thompson finished his day with 4min

30.55sec. It gave him a total of 8,707 points — 58 points more than Kratschmer who missed the meeting because it did not fit in with his training schedule for the European Championships in September 1982. But the fact that the reigning world record-holder had chosen not to defend in this tiny Austrian town can have made no difference to the outcome. Daley Thompson was driven on by ambitions — ambitions which drove him to reassert himself as the finest all-round athlete in the world.

Yet by the time that Thompson arrived in Athens for the 1982 European Championships he had not only lost that world record once more — he also found that it was another German, not Guido Kratschmer, who posed his greatest threat. Thompson went to Athens as Olympic and Commonwealth champion, looking to add the European crown — as a twenty-year-old in the previous championships of 1978 he threw away a big overnight lead and ended up with the silver. He also looked to regain his world title once more, for that had been taken from him just three weeks earlier by the giant Jurgen Hingsen. Hingsen stood 6ft 6in tall, weighed more than sixteen stones, and at twenty-four years of age enjoyed the company of a beautiful American girlfriend, Jeannie Purcell, who he had met in Pepper's Disco, Santa Barbara, during a winter's training in California. Hingsen and Thompson were the heavyweights of the European decathlon. It was a classic this-town-isn't-big-enough-for-both-of-us confrontation. Hingsen's world record was 8,723 points, compared with Thompson's former record of 8,704.

Daley Thompson set off at a furious pace in the boiling temperatures of the Greek capital. After three events, the Briton led by 167 — a big lead over the man who had taken his world crown only three weeks previously. The first event of that first day was the 100 metres. A time of 10.51 seconds gave Thompson 930 points; Hingsen took 802 points with 11.01 seconds. Then came the long jump. Thompson was again in front, his leap of 7.80 metres earned him a further 980

*Daley Thompson (G.B.) doesn't quite make it on this occasion.*

points; Hingsen again trailed with 7.58 metres and 937 points. In the shot Hingsen trimmed a handful of points off the Briton's lead. He threw 15.52 metres (819 points) to Thompson's 15.44 metres (815 points). But the decathlon is not decided after three events, however big a margin might have been built up. In the fourth event, the high jump, it was Hingsen's turn to rule supreme.

Thompson cleared 2.03 metres but then failed three times at 2.06 metres to leave himself with 882 points. Hingsen, meanwhile, summoned up his strength and went over four heights cleanly up to 2.09 metres, cleared 2.12 metres at the second attempt, 2.15 at the third, and in the space of one event had cut Thompson's lead by 101 points.

There was one event left that day and Thompson knew he had to pull back those points. He ran his 400 metres in 47.11 seconds, beating Hingsen by nearly one second, to end the day with a lead of 114 points and a total of 4,549, the fourth-best ever and knowing that the only three scores to have bettered it all led to eventual world records. Thompson had done the first part of his job well and only the high jump had let him down. Zeus, if he was watching, would have been impressed.

The 110 metres hurdles was the first event to be contested on the second day when Thompson edged further in front, clocking 14.39 seconds to the West German's 14.61 (916 points against 891). Then came the discus. This was the crucial event. Thompson messed up his first two throws and at that stage Hingsen only had to reproduce his best to clip 108 points off Thompson's lead. In the hurdles, Thompson was only eight-hundreths of a second outside his personal best after hitting the first two flights. Now he faced a similar situation and resolved it by throwing the discus one metre further than he had ever managed before. A throw of 45.48 metres gave him 790 points — thirteen more than Hingsen collected — and when he cleared 5.00 metres in the pole vault to gain 1,052 points to Hingsen's 1,005 with a vault of 4.80 metres, Thompson's gold medal was assured. His only battle now was for the world title.

Thompson was now just fifty points off the world record schedule. It was an amazing performance in these oven-like conditions and taking into account the intense pressure under which he had been placed over the previous four months, regaining his world record, then losing it again, and now being faced with the task of taking it back once more. His first attempt at the penultimate event, the javelin, resulted in a foul throw. His second did not pass the 60-metres mark and Hingsen went into the lead. But Thompson thrives on pressure. With his last throw he hurled the javelin 63.56 metres, three metres further than the German. That gave the Briton 8,111 points, a lead of 237 points over his arch rival. The gold medal was won — it had been virtually won since the end of the eighth event — but it now remained to be

seen whether or not Daley Thompson could summon up the will to take enough points from the 1,500 metres and regain the world record.

He needed a time of not more than 4min 26.5sec. His best was six seconds faster, but again there was a doubt. Would Thompson be capable after two days of energy-sapping competition which had begun at breakfast time on the previous day? Hingsen knew that this was one of his better events; he knew also that it was Thompson's least favourite, and for the first time the two giants had been drawn in the same heat. But Hingsen was not going to help Thompson strip him of his world record so soon. The pace was slow and for three laps Thompson, his lumbering style doing no justice to his handsome physique, trailed. It was just not fast enough, he was over three seconds behind schedule. Then, with some 250 metres to run, he launched himself, past one man, then another, until he was sprinting into the home straight. His time was 4min 23.79 seconds, enough to give him another 633 points. Added up they tallied 8,744 points — 21 ahead of Hingsen's brief record. Thompson was back. Too exhausted to do a lap of honour, he wrapped himself in a Union Flag and acknowledged the crowd. The man so often overshadowed by the likes of Ovett, who was not here, and Coe, who had failed that very day, was champion of the world once more.

# INDEX

140